Cultivating Resilience in Early Childhood

Written to support the use of the Thought Bubbles picture books, this guidebook has been created to help teachers and practitioners initiate 'nurturing conversations' and cultivate resilience in young children.

Early identification of mental health and wellbeing needs by those who spend the most time with the children is key to offering the support vulnerable children need. This series takes a proactive approach to mental health support, creating a culture of trust and resilience long before crisis point is reached. Based on the author's extensive research and wealth of experience, this guidebook will help start the conversation, showing the reader what to do and say early on in a child's life, to help influence the way that they experience the world in the future.

This book:

- Offers practical, low-cost actions that can be easily adapted to suit different environments and contexts.
- Explores key topics such as effective listening, communication, relationships and environments.
- Is designed to facilitate the effective use of the four Thought Bubbles picture books, supporting the practitioner to elicit nurturing conversations.

Designed to be used in a range of childcare settings, this book is an essential resource for all those who care for and educate young children.

Louise Jackson is a teacher, trainer and author who draws on her direct experience of working with children in schools to develop educational materials that are designed to promote participation, relationships and conversation. She has worked on 'closing the gap' projects with national charities, local authorities, schools, children's centres and training organisations to address educational disadvantage, finding new ways to build capacity and resilience across early childhood services and local communities.

Privileged to have worked alongside many inspirational teachers, practitioners and volunteers in educational settings where vulnerable children are thriving, Louise seeks to capture in her research and writing what it is that makes the difference for young children. Working in collaboration with illustrator Katie Waller, she has created a series of books and practical tools which will help local communities, parents, practitioners and teachers understand the valuable role they can all play in cultivating resilience in early childhood.

A practical guide for early years practitioners
and four children's picture books to
use with 4–6-year-olds.

Cultivating Resilience in Early Childhood

A Practical Guide to Support the Mental Health and Wellbeing of Young Children

LOUISE JACKSON

Routledge
Taylor & Francis Group

LONDON AND NEW YORK

Cover image credit: Katie Waller

First published 2022
by Routledge
2 Park Square, Milton Park, Abingdon, Oxon OX14 4RN

and by Routledge
605 Third Avenue, New York, NY 10158

Routledge is an imprint of the Taylor & Francis Group, an informa business

British Library Cataloguing-in-Publication Data
A catalogue record for this book is available from the British Library

Library of Congress Cataloging-in-Publication Data
Names: Jackson, Louise, 1964- author.
Title: Cultivating resilience in early childhood : a practical guide to support the mental health and wellbeing of young children / Louise Jackson.
Description: Abingdon, Oxon ; New York, NY : Routledge, 2022. | Includes bibliographical references and index.
Identifiers: LCCN 2021028275 (print) | LCCN 2021028276 (ebook) | ISBN 9781032135878 (paperback) | ISBN 9781003229988 (ebook)
Subjects: LCSH: Early childhood education--Psychological aspects. | Resilience (Personality trait) in children. | Child mental health.
Classification: LCC LB1139.23 .J34 2022 (print) | LCC LB1139.23 (ebook) | DDC 372.21--dc23
LC record available at https://lccn.loc.gov/2021028275
LC ebook record available at https://lccn.loc.gov/2021028276

ISBN: 978-1-032-13587-8 (pbk)
ISBN: 978-1-003-22998-8 (ebk)

DOI: 10.4324/9781003229988

Typeset in Antitled
by Deanta Global Publishing Services, Chennai, India

Access the Support Material: www.routledge.com/9781032135878

Contents

Preface

This book was written drawing on direct experience in schools and early childhood settings. Working as a deputy head in a primary school, teacher trainer and student at the Centre for Research in Early Childhood I was able to build on an action research project that began in 2015. I worked alongside a film company observing and editing extensive footage of child development from birth to five, young children who were learning in high quality, nurturing environments. As I watched over five hundred observational clips of the children learning and then interviewed early educators about their practice, it was clear that something special was taking place. Children who were considered to be 'at risk' and vulnerable appeared to be thriving. I set out to capture what had made the difference for these children initially to improve my own practice working with vulnerable children in a school. It was only when the coronavirus pandemic and school and nursery closures rendered more children 'at risk' and vulnerable it became clear that the findings of this project would be relevant to those working in education, health and social care with young children as part of the long term 'recovery and reconnection plan'. This project book and four accompanying picture books will support early educators and families to observe and notice indicators of mental health and wellbeing, to become proactive in their local communities, creating spaces and encouraging dialogue that will protect, cultivate and restore the resilience of young children.

Working alongside a talented children's illustrator, I was able to create a series of child-friendly picture books which could be used to prompt nurturing conversations with a child; to provide a creative approach for early educators to observe a young child's natural interaction and responses within a familiar play-based context. This enables the adult to feel comfortable, knowing what to say, when to say it and why. This simple approach encourages the child to take the lead in the conversation, to build their own narratives alongside each picture book, creating a physical and mental space to build relationships, talk honestly and build trust with someone who will listen and who is able to act on behalf of the child.

Anyone working with young children, including parents and older siblings, can support the development of a positive mindset, protecting and building mental health competencies from early childhood. This is not intended as a one-off 'intervention' nor is it a 'catch-up' programme for young children. It is about empowering the 'community' around a child to recognise the role they have in protecting and nurturing the mental health and wellbeing of the younger generation. 'It takes a village to raise a child' is an African proverb that describes how an entire community of people must interact with children for those children to experience and grow in a safe and healthy environment. This book is about shifting the discourse around mental health, changing the language particularly in relation to young children, birth to five. Moving beyond labels, gaps and deficits to build communities where protecting, growing and nurturing the mental health and wellbeing of all young children is seen as a priority, presents an opportunity for all those who care for and educate young children to find out what matters and what they can do.

Now, more than ever before, we are living in an 'age of anxiety'; and as a community we can either wait for a child to reach a crisis point before we take action or we can act early, teaching skills that will equip a child for life – a gentle process of restoring emotional balance, active listening and nurturing non-verbal and verbal communication that will help to build each child's resilience, restoring their trust in those around them. Each one of us has the capacity to create space, find our voice, make friends and think differently if we are surrounded by people who are prepared to listen, who understand why this is important, and who can support us in the process. This series of books will help you to start the conversation; knowing what to do and what to say early on in a child's life could change the way that a child experiences the world in the future.

Acknowledgements

I wish to extend special thanks to all my colleagues at Early Excellence, Vyka and Reel Learning who set me off on a journey of discovery into a child's early learning and development. I am grateful for the opportunity to study at the Centre for Research into Early Childhood, for the connections made through the British Early Childhood Research Association (Becera), Early Education and the Association for Professional Development in Early Years and for the many ways in which members of these organisations challenged me to revisit my values, ideas and beliefs.

The decision to put theory into practice and move from a training and consultancy role back to working in a primary school was never going to be easy, but I never imagined the significant challenges that lay ahead as the coronavirus pandemic closed schools and changed all our lives. I experienced first-hand the impact that recent global events have had on young children's mental health and wellbeing in my own school community and began developing and sharing educational materials working with schools, charities and communities in the UK. Working on international early childhood projects, meeting online with educators around the world to share experiences further raised my awareness of the wider impact on children's mental health, young children who were all watching, listening and learning from the people who care for them in their own communities. Many of these children have been deeply affected by their different experiences, and there is no doubt that their lives have been changed.

Now is the time to change the narrative; we have an opportunity and a responsibility to reimagine early education to focus on cultivating children's mental health and wellbeing. We can strive to build a community that prioritises the mental health and wellbeing of all our children. It is the children who thrive in spite of their difficulties who have much to teach us about resilience and survival in a crisis.

This book is dedicated to all the children who have shown me that you can:

Never underestimate the ability of a child.

Introduction

A child in mind

In March 2020, soon after his own primary school had closed due to the Covid-19 pandemic, Alex's parents requested a place in the 'emergency' school for keyworker and vulnerable children because his behaviour at home appeared to be spiralling out of control.

A vulnerable ten-year-old who struggled with social communication, Alex trusted his teacher and was able to articulate his fears to her. He explained that he felt frightened and was missing everyone. He didn't understand why he couldn't see his friends or why his mum was so upset. Over the next few weeks, Alex found new ways to express his feelings. He watched the news broadcasts about the pandemic and responded in a way that helped him to manage his emotions. He found that he could recreate the government scale of risk, using it to describe his own feelings of dysregulation. He colour-coded his scale of feelings to highlight his own danger zones. Alex drew a set of icons to illustrate a full range of feelings, all of which he had experienced during the first week of school closure; ranging from 'very angry', 'furious', 'panicking', 'slightly stressed' to 'just about OK!' (see Figure 0.1).

During a period of great uncertainty and change, Alex was especially vulnerable because circumstances beyond his control were impacting negatively on his mental health and wellbeing. Despite the events which threatened to engulf him, Alex showed that he could express his feelings clearly to someone he trusted and that friendships were especially important to him. With the support of sensitive adults, he was able to build resilience for future 'event horizons' using strategies that could be applied across different situations and throughout subsequent periods of high anxiety and stress.

Meanwhile, the youngest children were expressing their anxiety through their role-play, creating safe spaces to hide from the virus. Children were observed as they played with friends, running away and escaping whilst being chased by the emergency services, dressing up in masks to stop infection and building vehicles and machines to keep everyone safe. Children as young as four and five years old expressed their fears about their friends, family and teachers becoming ill and dying. The extreme strain on mental health and wellbeing was evident in children's talk and in their role-play. Notes posted in the class 'worry box' show the levels of anxiety and mix of emotions experienced by young children when concerns about a wobbly tooth are shared alongside concerns about infection, illness and death (see Figures 0.2–0.5).

Mental health in early childhood is important because children are telling us through their play, in their actions and conversation that they want and need to make sense of the world around them. They want to understand why the world has changed for them and what they can do to restore a sense of balance within themselves.

DOI: 10.4324/9781003229988-1

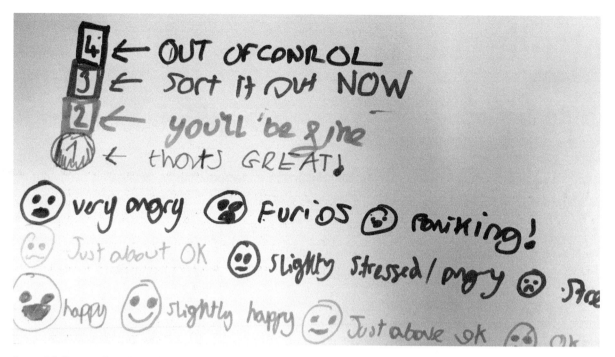

Figure 0.1 Emotional regulation from a child's perspective.

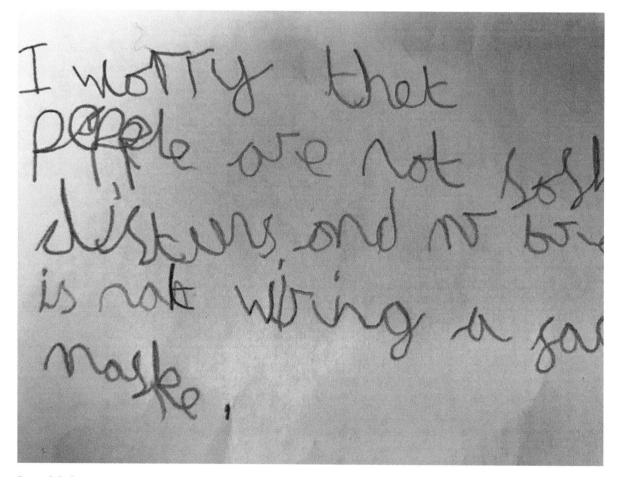

Figure 0.2 Expressing worries about infection control from a child's perspective: 'I worry that people are not social distancing and Mr Burns is not wearing a face mask'.

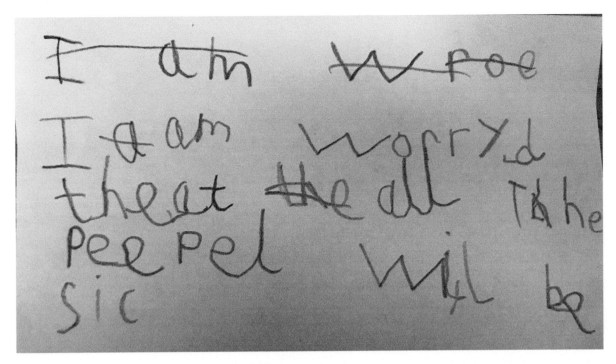

Figure 0.3 Expressing worries about illness from a child's perspective.

Figure 0.4 Expressing worries about death from a child's perspective.

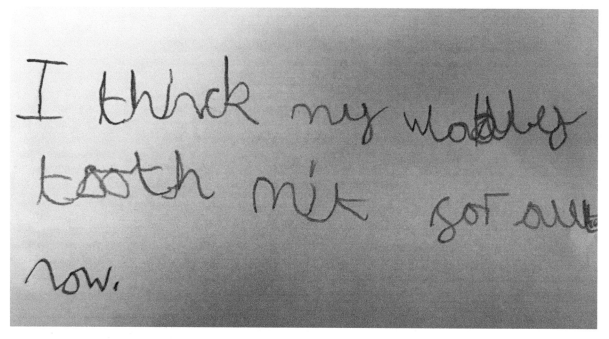

Figure 0.5 Expressing worries about a wobbly tooth from a child's perspective.

The ways in which we, as adults, observe, interpret and then respond to dysregulation in young children needs to be carefully considered because if we only react to surface behaviours, we may miss an opportunity for the child to learn from emotional co-regulation. Adults and children can work together to find ways to respond and resolve negative emotions which can then be used to help protect and enhance that child's ability to self-regulate and build 'realistic optimism' – resilience for the future.

Prevention and early intervention – a way forward?

The 'Age of Anxiety' described in the 1990s and examined in Jean Twenge's American research provides an historical and cultural context which has contributed to our understanding of children's mental health in the UK (Spielberger and Rickman, cited in Twenge, 2000). A new wave of anxiety amongst children caused by the Covid-19 global pandemic in 2020/21 has intensified our concerns for children's mental health and wellbeing, highlighting the increasing need for more information, research and practical advice.

The importance of mental health protection and early intervention which starts before the age of five provides the starting point for this book. The foundation for secure mental health is built early in life, as childhood events and experiences, including children's relationships with parents, caregivers, relatives, teachers and peers shape the architecture of the developing brain. Mental health problems can occur at any time throughout childhood, issues causing concerns about a child's anxiety or disruptive behaviour in the early years can sometimes increase the likelihood of the child experiencing a serious emotional disorder, depression or diagnosed mental illness later in life. When children are given early support to overcome these feelings of dysregulation, they have typically been the beneficiaries of exceptional efforts on the part of supportive adults. This book builds on a small-scale project which set out to capture these exceptional efforts of supportive adults when vulnerable children thrive, what early indicators were used, what actions were taken and why.

Research into practice

During 2020, 1.7 billion children in education were adversely affected by school closures and many young children across the world experienced loss and trauma because of the Covid-19 pandemic. The consequences of this will be different for each child and family, as each person has their own unique story to tell, building a collective narrative of events and experiences supported and facilitated by the sensitive interaction of exceptional parents, carers and early educators. The impact of this emotional instability and toxic stress on early brain development will continue to impact throughout a child's life. The Center on the Developing Child, Harvard University, is a strong advocate for early identification and action stating that 'Most potential mental health problems will not become mental health problems if we respond to them early' (Center on the Developing Child, 2013). We have both an opportunity and a responsibility to take preventative action if we are to change the trajectory for those young children who have been negatively impacted by the current pandemic.

Research into the disruptive impact of toxic stress in early childhood has been extensive and has provided an insight into the causal mechanisms that link early adversity to later difficulties in learning, behaviour and both physical and mental wellbeing (Shonkoff and Garner, 2011). The ability to manage stress and the neural processes that control the energy expended, to deal with the stressor and then recover, depends on a child's earliest exposure to adverse childhood experiences. When an individual's stress levels are too high, various systems for thinking and metabolic recovery are compromised. The signs of dysregulation show up in the behaviour or mood, or attention and physical wellbeing. A child who is suffering from stress cannot learn, so educational 'catch up' and 'recovery' programmes will need to take this into account.

The negative impact of the recent pandemic and sudden closure of educational settings on children could continue for many years to come unless there is an urgent focus on early education that prioritises mental health protection and care. It is more effective to treat young children's early dysregulation within the familiar contexts of their families, homes and communities rather than wait for negative feelings to escalate, increasing the need for clinical intervention and specialist support in later years. We have a unique opportunity to cultivate or 'grow' resilience, recognising and protecting a child's mental health competencies from an early age: parents, caregivers, relatives, teachers and peers working together to change outcomes for all our children. A strategy for prevention and intervention in early childhood which compliments and underpins the work of specialists in the field of mental health, a programme of positive action that can be delivered widely through universal early education and childcare and one which builds on the broad definition of self-regulation included the new UK early education framework. There are practical actions that all those working on the 'front line' of education can take to change the stress responses of vulnerable children, supporting co-regulation and leading to the acquisition of new coping mechanisms that will protect the child from future stressors.

What information is needed by early educators?

In many countries, schools and early childhood settings have the potential to take a leading role in the effective prioritisation of education/health funding to reduce the effects of toxic stress in early childhood. Extensive international aid programmes that focus on Learning through Play (LtP) are funded by UNICEF and The LEGO Foundation. It is a global strategy for prevention and early intervention that lies in our understanding, acceptance and implementation of the human rights of the child – the right to play.

When Learning through Play (LtP) practitioners working with the youngest children are trained to notice and identify children who may be at risk of emotional dysregulation, they can then use this knowledge to target early intervention and provide support. Layard and Hagell (2015) suggest that educators should measure pupil wellbeing regularly, that they should make the wellbeing of pupils an explicit objective and be trained so that they can notice and promote child wellbeing and mental health.

A universal screening for mental health in early years could double or treble the traditionally small numbers of children receiving the help they need at an early stage but this could have both positive and negative consequences. Whilst intervening early is beneficial for the child, it can be costly and specialist services may struggle to meet demand, especially in current circumstances. When children are 'diagnosed' too early there may be a potential for the false identification of difficulties before a child has developed neurologically, this might lead to negative labelling of children (Rowland, 2017). A review of the measurements used in previous studies and summarised by Szaniecki and Barnes (2016) identified a wide range of assessment methods that have been used in previous studies to assess mental health. Measurements include structured and semi-structured interviews with parents/carers, questionnaires, checklists and methods that look at the nature of parent–infant relationships. Many of the observational strategies described in the literature, require extensive training to administer and code and are more applicable for research than routine practice. Further research is needed to find out which observations and measurements of mental health are fit for purpose when used with children of four or five years of age (Cremeens, Eiser and Blades, 2006).

Instead of measuring a deficit, the measurement of wellbeing and mental health in schools and early years settings is recommended with a range of measurement tools being offered to suit different ages and stages. Further information on tools that can be used effectively with different age groups to measure mental health and wellbeing can be viewed here: www.AnnaFreud.org. However, it is not just about collecting data, it is how this data is *used* to make the changes that will positively impact and make a difference to a young child.

Early identification of health and wellbeing needs in children under five requires early childhood educators who are trained and skilled in observational assessment. Educators who are familiar with a consistent use of terminology and who can use a coherent framework for observation in a child's familiar playful environment rather than a clinical setting.

The criteria used to review a child's mental health and wellbeing is already familiar to educators working in the English education system and can be linked to equivalent terms in the literature used in previous studies involving young people. A glossary is provided at the end of the book to ensure a consistent, shared understanding of the terms used across the action research process and further tools are provided to support your own observations of children in an early childhood educational setting. These should be adapted to suit the context in which you are working.

What is vulnerability in early childhood?

There is a public misconception that the issues relating to mental health are irrelevant for younger children; recent news reports of increasing numbers of younger children self-harming have been both shocking and a stark reminder of a 'cry for help'. Young children returned to school showing signs of their anxiety in the form of tics, reports of nightmares, a regression in skills and in their play.

The vocabulary used in the literature review to define 'vulnerability' was varied, multi-faceted and sometimes confusing, the term is now used widely across communities to describe different scenarios and different people. The language of mental health and mental difficulties is often more commonly applied to older children, young people and adults. It could be argued that the act of obfuscating or obscuring the perception of vulnerability and risk using different terms prevents the collection of reliable data and masks the true picture of mental health and mental illness in early childhood.

A younger child is less likely to have a diagnosis than an older child in school, so educators may feel less certain about describing the child's mental health in concrete terms and will act cautiously to avoid misdiagnosis or negative labels and expectations. However, a focus on mental health competencies empowers early childhood educators to talk about mental health positively, prioritising it within their practice without the need for negative labels, specialist referrals or a diagnosis.

Once a child's mental health competencies have been identified, early educators need to know what low-cost practical actions can be taken to protect and nurture these capabilities within the early childhood setting or classroom. Clinical tests and interventions at this early stage are often not developmentally appropriate nor are they financially viable. In some settings where teachers described how a written referral took the place of practical early actions, educators were left feeling disempowered and frustrated by long waiting times for appointments. A child's inability to regulate their own behaviours and emotions alongside the adult's concerns often escalated during this 'waiting time' leading to a culture of negativity and hopelessness around the child. A change in approach, which empowers educators to act within the child's familiar play-based learning environment whilst waiting for further investigation was perceived to have the greatest impact on children's mental health and wellbeing.

As you read this book, it may be helpful to keep 'a child in mind', to help you to translate research into practice. Use it as an opportunity to observe and listen to children's 'real world' experiences using a different 'lens' which will ultimately help you to build a holistic picture of their mental health and wellbeing. As you read, it is important to remember this is *not* a book about diagnosing mental illness in young children. It is a book which will help you to find new ways to respond and *protect* the mental health of children.

Addressing the damage caused by traumatic events such as the pandemic in 2020/21, using a familiar, child-centred and developmentally appropriate approach to intervention, the quality and consistency of co-regulation experiences between an early educator and a child are important because each child's experience of co-regulation helps to build the neural pathways that regulate emotion. The plasticity of the brain before the age of five provides a window of opportunity for all those working with young children to focus on re-establishing neural pathways that encourage positive patterns of thinking, establishing new coping mechanisms that will change a child's response to stress and expressions of distress in the future.

Developmentally appropriate observations made whilst the child is at play, and which focus on the child's mental health risks *and competencies* will ensure that mental health strengths are recognised and mental health needs or 'gaps' are identified at an earlier age.

Who might use this project book and series of picture books?

Educators are encouraged to adopt a participatory pedagogy in which they look for the involvement, relationships and communication systems that enable the child to participate fully in early childhood education: a strategy of noticing and observing children at play that can be applied at home, in any educational setting or emergency school.

This book is relevant to anyone working directly with children, and those who support parents, carers and relatives, including older siblings, to educate and care for a child under five.

- Early childhood educators, teachers and practitioners.
- Parents and carers.
- Learning mentors, social workers and family support workers.

- Early childhood educators working in international education, education in emergency and refugee camps.
- Students, trainees and newly qualified teachers and practitioners – a programme for continuous professional development and training.

Whether you are working in an educational setting, home-based learning or an emergency education centre, the signs of emotional instability in children under the age of five will be similar. This is because the characteristics of effective learning, stages of child development and mental health competencies for children under five apply across cultures and contexts. They are not specific to a particular educational system or curriculum, they apply to children everywhere. The practical actions which are suggested in this book can be delivered across a local community, they are low-cost and easily adaptable to suit the context wherever you are working.

This project book is accompanied by a series of four children's picture books which can be used by a teacher, parent or practitioner to start a child-friendly 'serve and return' conversation with children about mental health and wellbeing. A set of rich illustrations designed to get children talking, an opportunity to translate research into practice and then reflect with others on the children's responses within your own working context and culture. The nurturing conversation is set within a familiar and enjoyable context for young children that feels 'safe' – sharing a book. The illustrations and limited text are designed to encourage open conversation, talking, signing or interaction which the child can lead. There are opportunities to build on each narrative with further role-play ideas to stimulate children's thinking and talking so you can continue to build your own understanding and observations of children in your setting.

Practitioners may choose to use the project guide and set of picture books to support specific work with a family or parent group. The books can also be used separately to facilitate discussion and scaffold parent–child interaction. Each book introduces one of four key messages to the young child about mental health and wellbeing that can stimulate further discussion and insight into what a child knows and can do.

The key messages are relevant to both the educator and the child and provide a framework for the delivery of high quality, consistent co-regulation:

- Create space – a place to be me.
- Speak out – a voice of my own.
- Find friends – someone to listen.
- Think differently – memories of change.

Whether you are leading a practical workshop or demonstrating an early childhood teaching approach, the books can be used with adults and children to illustrate and model practical 'serve and return' interactions that have been successfully used by early childhood educators to find out about and support the mental health and wellbeing of young children (see Figure 0.6).

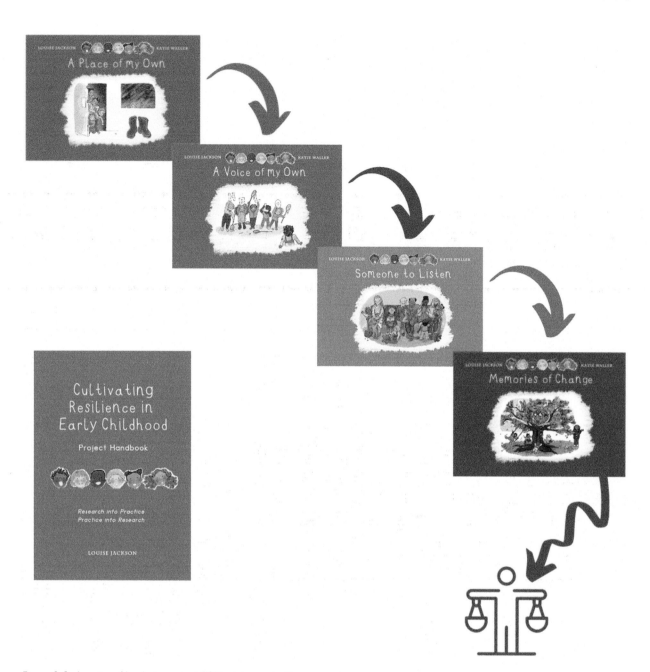

Figure 0.6 A series of books to support ECE training and action research.

1. Changing the 'at risk' trajectory

The Children's Commissioner of England produces local area profiles of child vulnerability, helping national government and local councils identify how many vulnerable children there are, highlighting groups at heightened risk, particularly during the coronavirus emergency. Vulnerable groups are those in overcrowded or inadequate accommodation, with fragile parents, young carers or without internet access. It became clear that there are hundreds of thousands of children in England who are living with multiple secondary risks that Covid-19 may exacerbate: lack of food in the house, homelessness or living in cramped living conditions, neglect, domestic abuse, substance abuse and parental mental health problems. As the UK entered a third period of lockdown and closure of schools, the increase in the numbers of children eligible to attend schools on the grounds of vulnerability demonstrated the impact the pandemic was having on children and their families across communities.

Children who are exposed to multiple socioeconomic risks in their early years are more likely to experience disadvantage in terms of their cognitive and behavioural development before starting school, highlighting the importance of early intervention in children's lives to break intergenerational cycles of disadvantage. (Allen, 2011; Tickell, 2011). When funding and intervention in the early years are determined by social and economic 'risk' children may become marginalised; they may be subject to low expectations and may be given a label to describe their needs. This label can be disabling for a child, it may be interpreted in different ways leading to confusion and misunderstanding.

In many countries children at risk have rightly been prioritised over others; an overarching strategy to address inequality and reduce the 'disadvantage gap'. Within the UK education system, vulnerable or 'disadvantaged' children have become a political focus for funding streams such as the 'Free School Meals', 'Pupil Premium' or, more recently, 'catch up' programmes. The reliable allocation of funding relies on effective communication and sharing of data across birth to five children's services, and with parents and carers. Whilst these strategies are well-intentioned, the reality for many families is that funding to support early intervention may be accessed too late, with missed opportunities to target funding when it can have the most impact – in early childhood.

In the UK the measure, or risk, of vulnerability for children starting school will only be recorded when a child is 'known' to children's health, education or social services; if parents make a choice not to reveal their economic status or the child has not yet been registered with health/social services they may be 'invisible' and unable to access the support and funding they are entitled to. This situation is exacerbated in a global pandemic where the definition of 'vulnerability' is constantly changing and means different things to different people. The issue

DOI: 10.4324/9781003229988-2

was described in the report 'Unknown children – destined for disadvantage?' (Ofsted, 2016) highlighting the necessity of joined up thinking and sharing of information across health, social and education provision for under-fives. In January 2021 official figures show 174,000 children were identified by social workers as living with domestic abuse, but the Children's Commissioner estimated that there were many more – as many as 789,000 children in this situation but who had not been identified by the system and who were likely to miss out on vital services (Longfield, 2021). Effective collaboration across health, education and social care services for families of children under five must be a priority for policy makers globally, the fragmentation of children's services has had a serious and negative impact on an early educator's ability to offer 'early help' when it is needed most. There is a risk that the needs of the 'vulnerable' in a global pandemic become impossible to manage unless we work together as a community with clear criteria and consistent terminology.

A formal screening process or system of identifying a child 'at risk' of vulnerability before they start school can be detrimental for the child. Early educators can be drawn into a deficit model from the start, focusing on what the child does not have and what they cannot do. So, the challenge for educators is to identify those children who need help without labelling the child; not easy when it is often the labels that provide access to funding streams and resources.

Children living in the most deprived areas start school with higher levels of mental health difficulties compared with the most affluent children, and this disparity widens dramatically over the first three years of school. In one Scottish study, the strongest predictor of having mental health difficulties at age seven years was having mental health difficulties reported at age four years, and there was a more than threefold widening of this disparity over time. By the age of seven years, children from the most deprived areas had rates of difficulties three-and-a-half times higher than their more affluent peers. Children's demographic backgrounds strongly predicted their age seven scores (using the Goodman's Strengths and Difficulties Questionnaire) but it was clear from this study that schools and settings made a significant contribution to mental health trajectories (Maryatt et al., 2018). If educators were equipped to identify those children at increased risk when they start in an educational setting, the children could be monitored carefully and additional support could be offered to narrow inequalities and change this trajectory.

A child's risk factors can be viewed as external or internal – whether the child is adopted or fostered, whether the family is on a low income, known to social services or known to have been exposed to violence, separation and loss. Internal risk factors might include birth trauma, postnatal medical needs, hidden disability or familial experience of depression, loss and separation. The information that is collected 'on entry' into early childhood provision from parents and carers sometimes provides details of these potential risk factors. Further information relating to concerns about a lack of food in the house, risks of homelessness or living in cramped living conditions, neglect, domestic abuse, substance abuse and parental mental health problems may become apparent during a home visit, but it is clear that this kind of personal information will only be shared within the context of a strong home/school early support network rather than with a stranger.

We have an opportunity to change the lens that we use to observe children in need, moving from a deficit model to a 'capability' observation model which focuses on the mental health competencies which really matter in early childhood, and which will lay the foundations for mental health and wellbeing in the future.

Parents and carers should always be given an opportunity to share family information if they want to; but early educators will need to have developed an open, honest relationship with families, helping parents and carers understand how this information is relevant for the education of their child, offering reassurance of confidentiality and trust. In some situations it may be appropriate to shift our focus away from 'risk' factors in the early years, especially when the information about a child is incomplete. Knowing about the 'risks' is helpful when working with young children, but the information will need to be contextualised, especially if it is used to determine the allocation of funding and resources. A targeted approach to 'risk' alone may no longer be useful or developmentally appropriate in the early years and may have limited success when funding and interventions are applied before children are able to articulate and express their own feelings (Wichstrom et al., 2012).

When practitioners are asked to select which observable characteristics provide them with the most valuable information about a child's mental health and wellbeing, they say that a holistic view of the child's capabilities is important. A wide range of observations are described (see Table 1.1).

A much clearer picture of the child's state of mind is seen when risks *are considered* alongside mental health competencies. A universal, child-centred approach is where young children are accepted, valued and given opportunities to engage in meaningful conversations with people they already trust. The child shows what they know and can do. When early educators implement a screening process that involves observation, interaction and dialogue with the child alongside collating the information gathered about risk factors, they can build a much more detailed picture of the child's overall mental health and wellbeing. The early educator can prioritise their attention, funding and resources to the children who need it most and at a time in their life when it will have greatest impact. The child becomes an active participant in the screening process, no longer dependent on someone else to notice and judge when and if mental health interventions are needed (Figure 1.1).

Table 1.1 Indicators Used by Research Participants to Assess Mental Health and Wellbeing

Mental health competencies	Representing objects	Sense of achievement	Making links	Managing feelings and behaviour
Persistence	Health and self-care	Involvement/ participation	Moving and handling	Having ideas
Curiosity	Making relationships	Communication signs/pictures/speech	Focus and concentration	Understanding
Self-confidence and self-awareness	Taking risks	Reviewing	Listening and attention	Wellbeing

Research into Practice

Focus groups of early childhood educators shared what actions they had taken to reduce stress and anxiety for children who were starting school or nursery for the first time.

Observing the children at play, they had taken note of what aspects of the unfamiliar 'environment' might have on individuals within the group.

"The outside space is crucial for children, but our outside space is really large so to begin with it can be overwhelming for children to see such an extensive space – we use portable fencing as a means to limit the space, so children become confident in one area before we introduce another."

"The children in our bilingual schools move fluently between the different languages, they choose which language to use with each educator. Children are confident to communicate, they have autonomy in the classroom and are building lifelong multi-lingual skills."

"We use online education tools to bridge the gap between home and school. When the school was closed, we quickly realised that the platform was going to provide an important channel of communication between parents and educators."

"It's made a massive difference having staff who speak other languages. Over the years we have evolved that so that initially those staff would be talking to children in the setting using the child's first language as much as possible but now we very much encourage both languages so whatever we are doing children hear it in Polish and hear it in English as well."

"The record of learning and development in photos, videos and observations showed continuity whether it took place in a home-based setting or in school. Educators at school and at home were able to see the 'flow' of learning during periods of school closure, creating important transition information that we could talk to children about and build upon."

Figure 1.1 Research into practice 1.

When is the right time to act?

The transition period from home into education has been described as a time of increased anxiety and stress for a child. It can be a period when mental health and wellbeing are challenged, put under strain or intensified for many young children; a time when their responses to anxiety and stress are made clearly visible. Many children during the 2020 pandemic were forced to move between education in a group setting to education isolated from their peers; a child who is subject to frequent illness or absence from education may likewise have to adjust frequently to different settings and expectations.

During a settling-in period, educators observe and notice 'event horizons' (behaviours that arise from a child's inability to emotionally regulate actions – anger, distress, anxiety or fear) and look for causative factors and triggers, recognising that these may be different for each child. An 'event horizon' occurs when a child reaches a point of no return – crying, shouting, falling to the floor due to a temporary loss of emotional and physical control. The intention of the early educator is not to establish a transition which is devoid of stress because this is not conducive for learning (Yerkes–Dodson Law), but to become aware of and manage different responses to stress within a safe and supportive learning environment. The transition phase when a child moves between home and an educational setting (or from an educational setting back to home as in the 2020 pandemic) is a critical point in a child's life that can be used to model co-regulation of emotion, helping the child to form new neural pathways and change their initial response to stress.

Whenever a child loses self-control, Shonkoff and Garner (2011) state that adults have a role to play in restoring a child's sense of control – thus reducing the physiological stress responses in young children. In a moment of change or transitional phase where a child is prone to increased anxiety or stress, a young child can be well supported by a parent, carer or an early educator to shift their stress response. When transition processes were disrupted or cancelled altogether, as they were in September 2020, specialist education services reported a significant increase in referrals for dysregulation amongst children aged four and aged eleven. This was experienced by educators working in early years settings and primary schools, children as young as three or four were seen self-harming, prone to violent outbursts or showing aggression towards parents and caregivers. The importance of the 'settling in' period during a time of transition between educational settings should not be underestimated.

The children described in the case studies were all able to change their responses to stress because of the sensitive interaction from supportive adults. It is possible to change the 'at risk' trajectory for young children when the indicators or signs are noticed and used as opportunities to co-regulate, establishing mental health competencies which build up resilience that will last a child's lifetime (see Figure 1.2).

Research into Practice

"We try and find out lots about the children, what the children like to do, things that they are interested in. We tend to use the information from the home visit to support the way in which we set up the environment."

Analysis of the research data over three years showed that children with special educational needs and disability (SEND) were consistently perceived to show lower levels of wellbeing and lower levels of involvement than their peers when starting school. Discussion with educators revealed that this was accepted by many educators as 'to be expected' and no further action was taken.

Where children with SEND were assessed as showing high levels of wellbeing and involvement the educators had taken practical actions to promote each child's wellbeing and involvement from the start.

 • Early Educators had sought information from home about the child's interests.

 • They had gained a better understanding about how the child showed happiness and what gestures might indicate a sense of achievement.

 • They established a relationship that enabled them to notice, interact and respond positively to each child's early attempts at communication.

"We may need the parent to stay and play alongside the child so they can become confident in the environment alongside someone they can trust."

"We notice how the child is choosing to communicate with us - using gesture, expressions, signs, objects of reference. If a child can communicate, they are going to find it easier to build a relationship."

"When we know we've got the environment right the children are happy and engaged."

'Exceptional' educators established a relationship based on trust from the start and created a culture that enabled them to notice, interact and respond positively to each child's early attempts at communication.

The child's wellbeing and mental health was prioritised during a time of change and potential anxiety.

Figure 1.2 Research into practice 2.

2. A new measure of risk and competency

The language of mental illness and mental difficulties is more commonly applied to older children, young people and adults, leading to a public misconception that the issues relating to mental health are less important for younger children. This is not the case.

The observations routinely made by educators when children start school in the UK can provide valuable information about the mental health of a child, especially when it includes indicators of both risks *and competencies*. When this information is collected and aggregated, it is possible to view trends and patterns that could be used to build a picture of the mental health of children aged four to five years across the school, the setting or across a geographical locality. An opportunity for stakeholders and funders to focus resources where they are needed most, building on what is working well rather than patching up the gaps.

Early childhood educators use observations in the classroom to find out how a child learns but may not always recognise these observations as important indicators of the child's mental health. Likewise, parents and carers are 'tuned in' to notice their child's behaviours or event horizons and are already familiar with the triggers and reactions that can lead to distress or anxiety. Observations are made whilst the child is 'at play', in the presence of familiar people and in familiar child-friendly environments. The term 'proximal development' refers to those skills that the learner is 'close' to mastering; when the child is engaged and at play, they are likely to be functioning at their full potential. The child feels safe, relaxed and able to function within their own zone of proximal development so observations are likely to give an accurate picture of what a young child already knows and can do.

When educators 'notice' a child's level of involvement or participation, the relationships (friendships) that are developed with peers and siblings and their use of communication to connect with others they begin to build a holistic picture of each child's competencies in terms of mental health. The breadth and quality of these observations will be more important than the use of a prescribed list or distinct measure, but it could also be argued that a shared list/collection of observations can help when working across an organisation or when training early educators in order to secure a consistent approach.

Early educators identified the following observable characteristics which can be used to make a judgement or provide insight into a child's health and wellbeing. All of these observations can easily be made within a play-based environment and do **not** require any formal assessment or test.

DOI: 10.4324/9781003229988-3

Observable characteristics which support the assessment of a young child's mental health and wellbeing are shown in Figure 2.1.

It is helpful to agree on a statement alongside each observable characteristic to clarify the meaning and ensure consistency. The observations are in line with the 2021 UK Early Years Foundation Stage curriculum framework, so educators will be familiar with the learning behaviours, explanatory statements and what to look for when observing young children.

It can be a useful exercise for educators working together to agree on their own definitions and guidance alongside the list, making it relevant to the context in which they are working. For example, it would be useful to consider whether health and nutritional information may already be provided by local health screening tools, whether a home visit or conversation with the parent/carer would give the relevant information or you may find it is clearly visible in the child's physical demeanour and oral health. The way in which a child shows curiosity will look different depending on the physical locality of the setting: urban or rural, in a school setting or temporary emergency centre, at home or in the nursery and so on. There may be value in charities and organisations using the list of observations to define their own set of guidance to collect relevant and consistent data about young children's health across a locality, region or country. In this way, a bespoke framework for screening, observing and noting a child's mental health and wellbeing is created without interrupting the child's play and interaction.

Observing the child's responses to the illustrations in the 'serve and return' books or linked role-play games can also be used by the educator to reflect against each criterion. All the observations will help to give an indication of a child's willingness to participate, their ability to interact, build relationships, communicate and use language to express themselves.

There is an opportunity to collect observational data by carrying out action research with the 'willing' participation of children. Educators take on the role of an 'attached researcher' seeking to build an accurate picture of each child's mental health risks and their mental health competencies. It takes time to really observe a child, noticing how they respond over different situations, with different people and in different places. The role of the observer is to stand back, watch, listen and to know when and how to respond, noticing when mental health competencies occur and when they do not, to build the holistic picture of the child.

Children who need help to build mental health competencies can be identified and prioritised within their first years of schooling, they can be well supported to shift emotional responses before negative feelings escalate or become embedded.

MENTAL HEALTH & WELLBEING IN EARLY CHILDHOOD

 Piece together the information you have about the child.

 Build a relationship & observe interactions with others.

 Observe the child's play and exploration. Look, listen and notice.

1 HEALTH & NUTRITION
Familiarise yourself with the risks that could occur in your community. Consider the network of support around the child. What are the opportunities, risks and who is available to help the child?

2 ENGAGEMENT IN PLAY
Observe a child interacting playfully with objects around them.
Does the child show curiosity, creativity and critical thinking?

3 RELATIONSHIPS
Observe a child interacting and communicating with others whilst playing.
What verbal/non verbal systems are used support effective communication?

4 SYMBOLIC PLAY
Observe a child engaging in symbolic play, using objects in role play to re-enact familiar experiences.
Does the child make links between objects, words (nouns) and functions?

5 PERSISTENCE
Observe a child struggling to interact playfully with an object that requires problem solving.
Does the child show perseverance when solving a problem?

6 FOCUS AND CONCENTRATION
Observe a child's focus and concentration when engaged in play and exploration.
Does the child show high levels of involvement?

7 CONNECTIONS
Observe a child making physical connections in construction play, and connecting a series of events or ideas.
Does the child show an interest in joining up objects, linking ideas, words and pictures.

8 EMOTIONAL LITERACY
Observe a child expressing emotion through their actions, words or signs.
Does the child communicate their emotions effectively? How do you know what they are feeling?

9 SELF-AWARENESS
Consider self awareness in terms of space as well as relationships.
How does the child move, negotiating obstacles and people? Then, consider the child's communication, listening and attention skills.

10 SELF-REGULATION
Notice what happens when the routine changes, when there is an unexpected event or intervention.
How does the child respond? What triggers an 'event horizon? How is the balance restored?

11 RISK-TAKER
Observe a child's movement across obstacles – moving on, over, under and through challenging environments. Does the child show stability? How does the child respond to risk?

12 REFLECTION AND REVIEW
Observe a child recalling a series of fictional or real events, describing people and places.
Does the child ask or answer questions, make choices and express preferences?

Figure 2.1 Mental health and wellbeing checklist.

Addressing mental health difficulties for those who need it, and promoting competence for all, is a key area for future consideration and research in Australia (Australian Early Development Census, AEDC 2018). There is an opportunity to build on a model used in Australia when children start school which was developed from research using the early childhood census data. The adapted model makes use of both risk factors and mental health competencies to identify diverse groups within a cohort of children. When the model was applied to the UK data, different groups within a cohort were identified and the adapted model clearly showed that some children do not reach 'at risk' thresholds but may still need support in the early years to protect and build their mental health competency for the future (see Figure 2.2).

When viewed from this perspective the children who have substantial risk and low competence (bottom right in the diagram) are identified as a distinct group which can be prioritised for practical and prompt action within their familiar early learning environment. A second group of children, who might easily get 'missed', were identified using this model but who can be described as having 'low' mental health competency (bottom left in the diagram). Adults working with these children need to be aware that if they are proactive, using everyday opportunities to show co-regulation and offer coaching in emotional literacy that they are helping those children to protect and build up their resilience for the future. Establishing a solid foundation of mental health and wellbeing in early childhood that will last a lifetime (Figures 2.3 and 2.4).

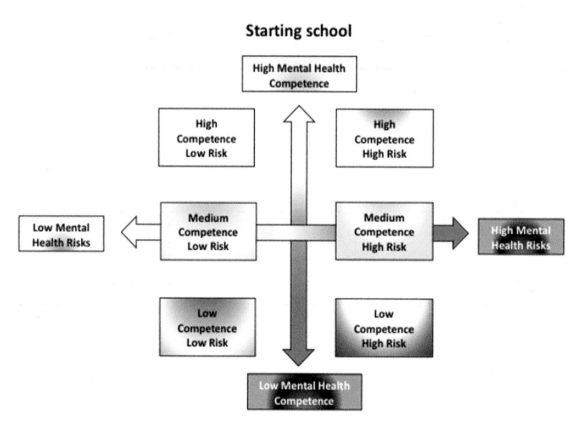

Figure 2.2 Model of risk and competency.

Research into Practice

MENTAL HEALTH & WELLBEING IN EARLY CHILDHOOD

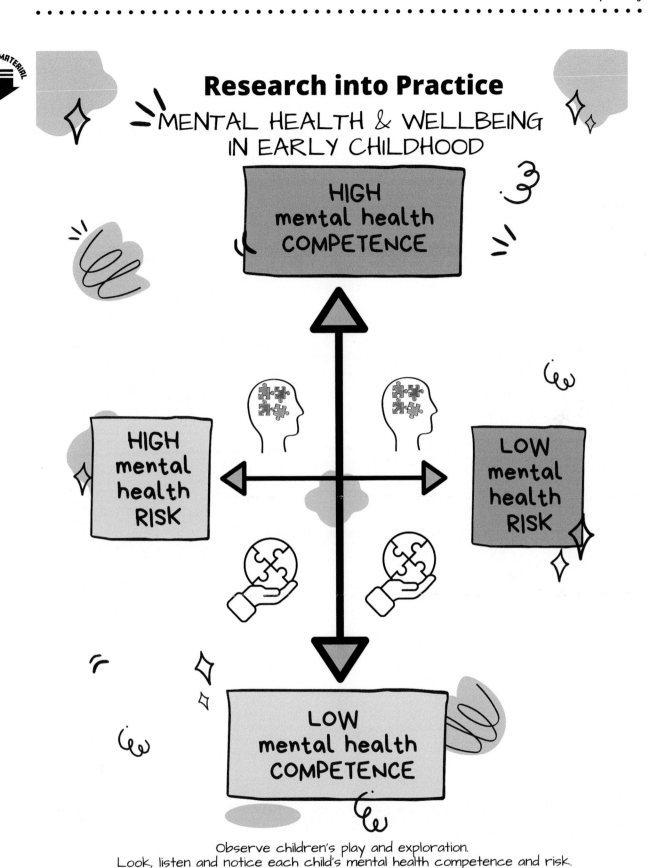

Observe children's play and exploration.
Look, listen and notice each child's mental health competence and risk.
Protect and build a child's mental health and wellbeing from the start.

Figure 2.3 Research into practice 3.

Research into Practice

Reflect on each child's mental health risk and competencies to highlight children who fall into each quartile of the model. Notice those children who are not 'at risk' but who have low mental health competencies. These are the 'invisible' children who could benefit from early intervention and support.

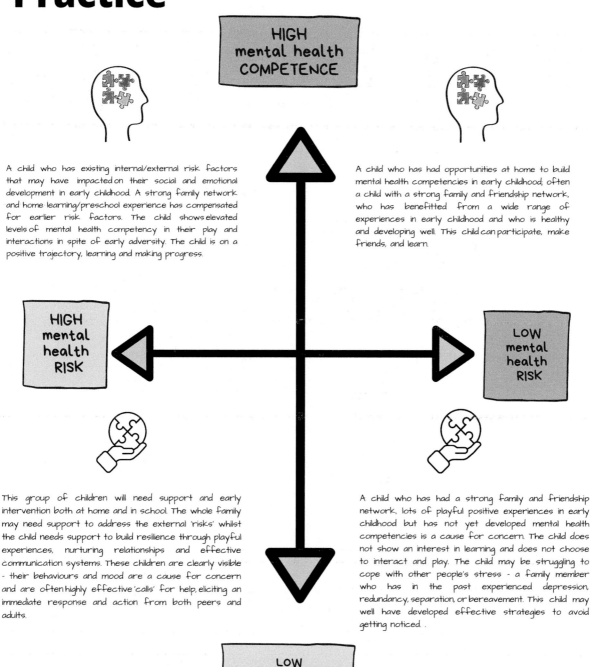

HIGH mental health COMPETENCE

A child who has existing internal/external risk factors that may have impacted on their social and emotional development in early childhood. A strong family network and home learning/preschool experience has compensated for earlier risk factors. The child shows elevated levels of mental health competency in their play and interactions in spite of early adversity. The child is on a positive trajectory, learning and making progress.

A child who has had opportunities at home to build mental health competencies in early childhood; often a child with a strong family and friendship network, who has benefitted from a wide range of experiences in early childhood and who is healthy and developing well. This child can participate, make friends, and learn.

HIGH mental health RISK

LOW mental health RISK

This group of children will need support and early intervention both at home and in school. The whole family may need support to address the external 'risks' whilst the child needs support to build resilience through playful experiences, nurturing relationships and effective communication systems. These children are clearly visible - their behaviours and mood are a cause for concern and are often highly effective 'calls' for help, eliciting an immediate response and action from both peers and adults.

A child who has had a strong family and friendship network, lots of playful positive experiences in early childhood but has not yet developed mental health competencies is a cause for concern. The child does not show an interest in learning and does not choose to interact and play. The child may be struggling to cope with other people's stress - a family member who has in the past experienced depression, redundancy, separation, or bereavement. This child may well have developed effective strategies to avoid getting noticed. .

LOW mental health COMPETENCE

Figure 2.4 Research into practice 4.

3. The provision of physical and mental space

Observational assessment is often misunderstood, it relies on an understanding that the balance of power between the 'giver' of data (the child) and the 'gatherer' of data (observer) is fragile. The data that is produced from sensitive observation of a child at play is far more valuable than any online test or questioning, the child's responses are natural, spontaneous and real.

Observational assessment is an important skill which requires in-depth knowledge about how children learn. When educators do it well, the information collected is of far greater value and more developmentally appropriate than any written checklist or screen-based test because it shows what the child can do; there are no pre-determined limits. When you consider the list of observations which are relevant to a young child's mental health and wellbeing described in Chapter 1, these are all clearly visible when a child is at play – no test is needed.

Educators highlight the need for a physical space to carry out observations and initiate 'nurturing conversations' with children about their feelings, responses to stress and coping mechanisms. The use of physical 'space' to support dialogue between adults and children and promote emotional wellbeing has been well documented and often relates to natural, outside spaces. The benefits of natural, outdoor space are particularly relevant when considering the emotional health of younger children, there has been much research on this that led to the widespread introduction of forest schools in the UK, Europe and Scandinavia. Creating space for outdoor play and exploration supports children's mental health and wellbeing and is an essential part of early years education. During the 2020 pandemic in the UK there were missed opportunities to move early childhood education and learning from school buildings and settings into outdoor spaces, increasing access to forest school sites and creating new ones. The photographs show the possibilities when just a small area of outdoor land is set aside for children to take over (see Figures 3.1–3.6).

Educators describe how they create their own physical spaces for children to think and talk, naming these spaces as the 'birdhouse', the hub, friendship tents and tipis. In each case, the child is given a choice about when to use the space, what to say (if anything) and what they want to do.

The layout in classrooms should also support the provision of a physical 'gathering' space to talk. A circle of chairs, benches or cushions provides children with a sense of equality where adults and

DOI: 10.4324/9781003229988-4

Figure 3.1 Space to reflect.

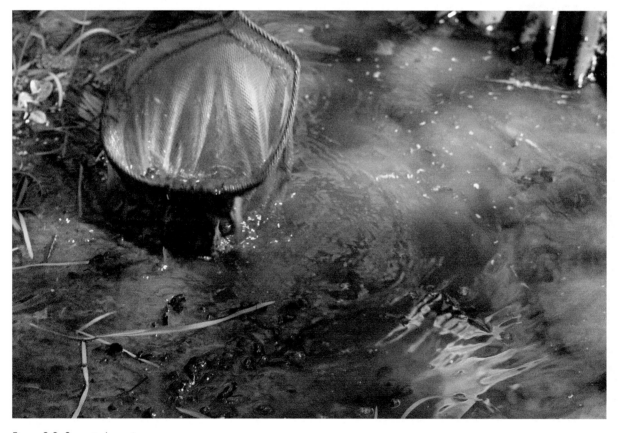

Figure 3.2 Space to be curious.

Figure 3.3 Space to play.

Figure 3.4 Space to connect.

Figure 3.5 Space to be independent.

Figure 3.6 Space to be still.

children meet, sit together, listen and talk to each other. When desks are in rows or space is limited in a classroom there are missed opportunities to observe children at play; the practitioner who is based at the front of a class is unlikely to notice when a child withdraws from the group conversation and may not notice the one child who is reluctant to participate. It might just be a fleeting observation, but it might show a great deal about the child's participation, relationship with others and communication (see Figures 3.7–3.10).

During the project, over 500 clips of observational video footage were collected and edited showing children from six months to six years interacting at home and in educational settings. Children were observed finding their own 'spaces' like those that the adults had described. The space was different for each child, ranging from the mud kitchen (an outdoor role-play area), a tipi tent to a woodland garden. There were common features that seemed important to every child; all the spaces had been initially chosen by the child themselves, had an element of familiarity (linked to home or earlier experience) and all were places where the child had autonomy, choosing when to go, and whether to engage with others or be solitary. For some of the children it was a place to practise new coping mechanisms where they felt safe and secure. Handing over the balance of power to the child, represents a culture shift in the relationship between the educator and pupil in educational settings. This is an important experience for children who may not have enjoyed this kind of autonomy previously due to their vulnerabilities. When the balance of power is shifted in this way across different contexts, a feeling of empowerment becomes part of the child's lived experience or memory.

One intervention approach encourages a young child to imagine or remember a 'physical space' where they feel happy and safe; the child learns to repeat the visualisation creating their own virtual or mental space which might then act as a coping mechanism for stressful situations in future. By building a mental picture of a favourite place, the sights, sounds and smells of a favourite beach, a garden swing or sitting under a special tree, you are helping the child to set up a positive memory that makes them smile. One they can return to in their imagination in the future.

The 'Serve and Return' books are designed to provide a 'virtual space' to explore thoughts and feelings. They can be used anywhere (in any space) to initiate a conversation whether the educator is working on their own with a child or encouraging group discussion. The picture books and follow-on role-play support a young child to practise visualising an imaginary space that makes them feel good, teaching them a coping mechanism that could be used in the future to escape negative thoughts and bad feelings (Figure 3.11).

Figure 3.7 A gathering space – to work together.

Figure 3.8 A gathering space – to work together.

Figure 3.9 A gathering space – to talk together.

Figure 3.10 A gathering space – to play together.

Research into Practice

A four-year-old who was expecting a move from the UK to South Africa used the role-play to express his anxieties about leaving his home and school. His teacher responded by placing a pair of golden gumboots in the role play area so that he could go on regular 'exploratory' trips using the golden gumboots; he was able to make new discoveries, rehearse conversations with new people and move out of his comfort zone from the safety of his familiar setting. Gradually, in his own time and at his own pace he was coming to terms with a meaningful change in his life and an approach that helped him to visualise and shift his thinking about an event that was causing anxiety.

A group of reception children who returned to school after a prolonged period of lockdown worked together for several days creating enclosures to 'Keep them safe' using wooden blocks. There was a sense that children needed to build walls around themselves, this was observed and noted. When the enclosures were used to stimulate role play the children were able to step out of the enclosure into the unknown using their imagination. There was always the choice to return and step back into the enclosure, but in practice the 'outside world was far too exciting to do that! Each child found themselves in a different imaginary place – jungles, forests, beaches, mountains and the 'stories' became more and more vivid as they honed their skills at visualising a different place.

One intervention approach encouraged a young child to imagine or remember a 'physical space' where they felt happy and safe; the child learns to repeat the visualisation creating their own virtual or mental space which might then act as a coping mechanism for stressful situations in future. By building a mental picture of a favourite place; the sights, sounds and smells of a favourite beach, a garden swing or sitting under a special tree, you are helping the child to set up a positive memory that makes them smile. One they can return to in their imagination in the future.

Figure 3.11 Research into practice 5.

4. A participatory pedagogy

'He just stands on the edge, silently watching the others, reluctant to join in. It is as if he is afraid of the other children'. Many educators will be familiar with a child like this, an observation which is especially poignant when continuous provision is set up and other children are showing elevated levels of involvement. The children who struggle with mental health and wellbeing in the early years are often those who find it difficult to make friends, initiate a conversation or join in playful learning.

Participatory pedagogy is a pedagogical approach in which the child is encouraged to find their own voice to express their thoughts and emotions. Children are given time and space to examine the relationships and environments that support learning from different perspectives. Participatory pedagogy enables young children to have a 'voice', providing an enabling environment with lots to talk about *and* with someone to talk to who will listen.

Children's rights have, like mental health and wellbeing, become an important part of policy and academic discourse, particularly since the ratification of the United Nations Convention on the Rights of the Child (UNCRC) (UN, 1989) by most countries in the world including the UK. Article 12 of the UNCRC gives children the right to have a 'voice' in all matters affecting them. Mental health in early childhood is intricately linked to children's rights, participatory pedagogy is the way in which we can ensure a child's rights are respected, recognised and met.

The teachers involved in this project were skilled in sensitive interactions, reflecting on them, thinking about them, and reconstructing them as a habitus. Reconceptualising the child as a person, not someone waiting to be a person is even more relevant for those who may have been subject to adverse childhood trauma, events that may have left them feeling disempowered and lost. A child who has been subject to medical investigations, displacement or bereavement will often have had little 'say' in what happened, they may have learned to passively accept what others say and do to them without question or protestation. Children in crisis, who have experienced these adverse childhood experiences may be unable to show emotion, they may be seen staring into space, turning away or rocking back and forth in a dazed state. Any small action that acknowledges their presence can trigger a response, actions might include saying or singing the child's name, making eye contact, a simple touch or offering an open hand.

Some children who have experienced adverse early childhood experiences struggle with joint attention, particularly where a parent or caregiver has suffered from depression, sensory difficulties or other issues that have affected early development of childhood interaction and communication. Effective participation

DOI: 10.4324/9781003229988-5

depends on children giving their joint attention to a shared experience. If it has not developed in early childhood naturally, educators need to set up opportunities to develop and practise it. Sharing a book and oral storytelling can be one way to develop joint attention with a child, encouraging participation and engagement with one other person whilst talking, reading and playing.

This links to 'Change Ideas' (Roberts, 2015), where the most vulnerable and disadvantaged children can be changed, via education. Children are supported to develop and express their views, and these are listened to and taken seriously. The protection of mental health is intricately linked to participative pedagogy; those concerned with child wellbeing and children's rights are concerned with seeking improvement in children's lives (Lundy, 2007).

Adults take participatory pedagogical actions in line with the age and maturity of the child, and this is made visible in the video footage where stories, games, role-play, pens, paper, paint and small-world play are used by teachers to encourage a child to express themselves and use their voice. The idea that a child 'at risk' and with 'special needs' can become a child with 'special rights' is an idea explored in the preschools of Reggio Emilia, a town in Northern Italy from which a pedagogical approach emerged in the aftermath of World War Two, and one which is based on an image of the child as rich in potential, strong, powerful, competent and most of all, connected to adults and other children.

An enabling learning environment with a layout and resources that encourage participation and involvement can support a child's mental health and wellbeing. Once in that enabling learning environment, educators can support a child's participation by first noticing them, quietly getting alongside to give a gentle physical or verbal prompt to involve them in the game. There is never a requirement for all children to become the 'life and soul of the party'; drawing attention to a child who is reluctant to use their voice or who cannot communicate easily is likely to lead to further withdrawal. Many of the children involved in the project prefer quiet focused involvement with one other child or a trusted key person and this is often all that is needed to draw in a child, helping them to find their 'voice' and start to make connections with their peers and supporting adults.

The 'Serve and Return' books in the series are designed to support this participatory pedagogical approach, encouraging young children to practise using their 'voice', spoken or signed, to express their thoughts and emotions in a safe space where they feel comfortable and know that they will be heard. Once the early years educator has practised using the approach with these four books, he/she will be familiar with the process; facilitating a nurturing conversation in which the child takes the lead can be repeated across different situations in school and at home (see Figure 4.1).

Research into Practice

Have you ever noticed the child who stands at the side and watches?
Staring vacantly into space,
showing little emotion and no interest
in spite of your best efforts to inspire and engage them.

In a busy, early years setting these are the 'invisible' children that can get missed – they follow the rhythm of the day, moving purposefully to avoid conversations with adults and resisting any temptation to join in the play with their peers. A child who appears to be 'alone' despite being in a group of children will struggle to learn and will need the support of sensitive adults to help them to feel safe. Some children may feel lost in an open-ended learning environment, especially when given a choice of what to do and who to play with.

 A sensitive adult will guide them around each area of the provision – giving time to look, listen and touch the resources. This is an opportunity to find out the child's interests, mirror the child's actions and where possible engage in turn taking play.

 At first encourage a child's non-verbal communication by responding positively to facial expressions and gestures – a smile, eye contact or a gentle touch can make all the difference to a child who is feeling vulnerable. Use the child's name, get down to the same level and provide physical or verbal prompts to promote participation in the play. Focus on the areas of provision that are familiar to the child – domestic role play, small world, or block play. The vocabulary you use will be familiar to the child and can be generalised across home and school.

 The use of visual support to organise resources enables children to be independent, make choices and get involved in play even if they are reluctant to speak. Use silhouettes, objects and photographs across the continuous provision to label and organise resources. Sequencing events during the day helps young children to know what is happening and what is coming up next. A 'first' and 'then' photo board can help children to understand regular routines at mealtimes and reassure them at the end of the day without the need for spoken language.

Once you have established a relationship, and the child begins to communicate with you; the teaching is to repeat, model and extend the child's language and actions alongside their play. For the reluctant speaker, making connections between actions, words and objects is a crucial step in the development of early language and an important way of building relationships.

- Make the most of all the opportunities in your continuous provision to engage the child in conversation.
- At this stage in a child's development, learning new vocabulary in context is far more meaningful than delivering a prescribed language intervention programme outside the early years classroom.
- 'Recognise the teachable moments' within the routines and rhythms of the day.
- 'Show, explain, demonstrate, explore ideas, encourage and question.
- 'Provide a narrative for what children are doing, facilitating, and setting challenges'
- Use open ended questions like 'I wonder…?' 'Can you…?' and 'Is it possible…?' giving the child lots of time to think and respond.
- Some children may need up to ten seconds of thinking time to process information and of course when they respond they may choose to express themselves in many ways, not just language.
- Recognise and acknowledge the way each child chooses to communicate, understand and accept when they choose to remain silent because this is important when building confidence and self-esteem.
- Build a 'Listening Culture' that empowers every child to use their 'voice', to communicate effectively using words, signs, gestures, expressions and the expressive arts.

Figure 4.1 Research into practice 6.

5. A listening pedagogy

A listening pedagogy describes an enabling environment where there is an openness and sensitivity to listen and be listened to. 'Listening not just with our ears, but with all of our senses including sight, touch, smell, taste, orientation'. An enabling environment that encourages listening means there must be time to be silent, to pause and to listen to each other.

Adults support children's mental health when they acknowledge their role as a listener and observer, as people who stand and watch, waiting for the right moment to intervene giving children time to communicate and express themselves. Educators describe the holistic approaches they take to create a listening culture in their schools and settings, building on positive relationships with both the child and the whole family.

Children in the observational video footage were given plenty of time to communicate, they were able to express views in a variety of ways (not just verbal) and these views were heard, actively listened to and acted upon by the adults in the classroom. Children were given opportunities to rehearse conversations that may cause anxiety or embark on conversations that might feel risky, without judgement. One child talked about a close relative who had become seriously ill and died, other children joined in sharing their own experiences of death. As a group, they reached their own conclusion about how death makes you feel sad for a while but then you remember good things, changing memories can help manage the sad feelings so that they get overtaken by better memories. Another child explained that her biggest fear was running out of food; she had previously lived in a remote Congolese village, and this was a real possibility. Thinking about what the family would do and talking about how the situation impacts every member of the family did not eradicate the risk, but it did enable the child to articulate the fear and then move on in her thinking. Sometimes discussion about sensitive subjects can be quickly shut down or controlled by adults, leaving children with the perception that certain subjects are 'off limits'. This can cause long-term damage, especially when a young person faces difficulties in later life and feels unable to speak about them openly. Research has shown that talking about a difficult subject is unlikely to arouse an unhealthy interest in the subject, instead it introduces vocabulary and accurate information to dispel myths and misconceptions.

Role-play, story books and small world play provided young children with opportunities to 'play out' uncomfortable situations to understand them better. When children returned to school following the period of lockdown their role-play focused on 'safety' – making the house safe so that the 'pretend' family could withdraw into this safe space, vehicles were designed to transport food safely with 'grabbers' to avoid contamination. As children played out their experiences some of the misconceptions that had developed over recent months became clear. One child thought that people wore a mask because they were infected – imagine his alarm when he saw friends, relatives and increasing numbers of people wearing masks; he thought they were infected and likely to become extremely ill or die in front of him. A frightening

DOI: 10.4324/9781003229988-6

misconception that was important to address for the child to feel safe. Another child thought his school was closed because all the staff had contracted the virus, he had not understood why the school had shut so suddenly, and nobody had given him any reason to think differently. Tuning into what children are thinking is essential if we are to address their concerns and worries, watching a young child at play is just a different form of 'listening' and is a highly effective way of finding out what is on a child's mind.

The educators in our study were skilled in using active listening techniques in their interactions, they were able to show each child through their actions that they had been heard and taken seriously. Techniques included commenting on a child's play, mirroring, mindfulness, repeating and reflecting during conversation, giving sensitive physical and verbal support when needed. Daily mindfulness exercises, breathing games and peer-to-peer back massaging were all used with young children to reduce stress and model active listening.

Some examples of the sensitive interactions might include:

Giving a **commentary** about what is happening for the child,
describing or naming the emotion:
"I can see you are feeling angry/sad/frustrated".

Mirroring a child's actions, gestures and facial expressions
sends the non-verbal message:
"I'm feeling sad too".

Affect mirroring helps the child to
articulate their thoughts and emotions:
"I understand how you feel,
it is hard to forgive/forget when someone
has done that to you ...".

Encouraging mindfulness – gives the child space and permission
to consider their own feelings.:
"Describe what you are feeling right now".

Social stories retelling the story of an experience or event in words and/or pictures.

Reflecting on what happened before, during and after the event.

Repeating and **reflectin**g what the child has said can ease further discussion:
"I heard you say you are feeling angry ...".

Repeating and encouraging **reflective thinking** and **talking**:
"So, you are feeling angry, why do you think you are feeling like that?".

It was clear from the research discussion forums that adults can offer support and intervene if they have good levels of wellbeing themselves. If the educator or parent is consumed by anxiety and worry, then the child will need someone else to step in and give that level of support. Where the educators and caregivers are calm (using a quiet, slower pace of speech, limiting vocabulary and offering supportive non-verbal cues) they can restore a child's balance of emotions just by being present.

It is vital to remember that stress is contagious; if the educator can keep a sense of stillness during a child's event horizon (temper tantrum) this will have a positive impact on the child, helping to 'contain' their frustration rather than escalating it. A sense of stillness and calm, breathing deeply and in unison will reassure the child, restoring the balance and reducing levels of stress.

Children learn best at mid-levels of stress; too much stress and a child may become overloaded and will withdraw altogether or react with aggression, too little stress and a child can become passive and complacent. Just enough and the child is given an opportunity to develop a growth mindset, finding new ways to change their own stress responses and self-regulating behaviours. When considering mid-levels of stress, it is important to recognise that the optimum level of stress will be different for each child. The educator, parent or carer is often best placed to see and listen carefully to find the 'tipping point' for each child.

Physical closeness may be viewed by some children (particularly those who are neurodiverse) as a threat, so sensitivity is needed when a child is under stress. Likewise, when considering early childhood education during a pandemic, physical separation is necessary to slow down the progression of the virus, whilst responsive physical and social interaction is essential for strengthening resilience. Maintaining a focus on practicalities, using the term 'physical' distancing rather than 'social' distancing might help a child understand what they need to do and what social interactions are still possible, and which can still be enjoyed safely.

As parents and caregivers, we must look to reconcile these conflicting necessities through play and sensitive interactions at home and in an educational setting.

Reading a book together provides an opportunity for a parent and child to share a 'serve and return' interaction that is constructive, building the relationship that is needed for ongoing intervention and support: linking human mind to human mind, practicing mentalisation within a developmentally appropriate context.

Each 'serve and return' book is designed to be read aloud, with plenty of time to talk about the pictures on each page. Maintaining social connections using stories can help parents and caregivers to build a responsive relationship with a child. Stories about familiar children doing ordinary activities, creating a link between children and their friends which will help to reduce the effects of ongoing stress. Children are encouraged to identify with the different characters, sharing their own experiences and afterwards pursuing their own line of enquiry using the book as a catalyst for role-play, small world and further conversation. All the 'serve and return' interaction techniques mentioned in this chapter can be rehearsed through the medium of storytelling, especially when stories are accompanied by role-play, puppets and props.

6. Nurturing environments

Setting up a suitable environment that supports a child's emotional health and wellbeing is a key focus for all early educators. Wherever children are thriving, practitioners have worked hard to create a safe space, a place to think, talk and learn. After many years working with schools and early years settings, trying to decide what the characteristics of a nurturing classroom might be, the conclusion is that you do not see it; you feel it (see Figure 6.9 at the end of this chapter).

When you remember that stress is contagious, addressing levels of anxiety amongst the staff team will always have a positive impact on children's behaviour and learning. Regular supervision and coaching for early educators can be an effective intervention that does not involve direct contact with the child. In one school, a psychologist met with each member of the staff team every term. A dedicated period for the adults to reflect on children's learning, resolve issues and raise concerns. Working together, the educator and psychologist shared their combined knowledge and expertise to create a nurturing environment appropriate for each child. It was an ongoing 'pedagogical conversation' over the academic year that had far greater impact on children in the setting, one which empowered the practitioner to take responsibility and act.

The nurturing environment needs to be flexible so that it can become whatever the child needs it to be – a haven of safety (the friendship tipi), a place of familiarity (a book area) or a place of high or low sensory stimulation (a sensory room, or dark room). The role of the educator, parent or carer is to use their in-depth knowledge of the child to set up the learning layout and offer stimulating resources, adding enhancements and provocations based on the observations they have made, and the interactions they have had with the child and family.

Is it possible to consider a nurturing environment from a child's point of view? Children in one school were asked to look back on their experiences in primary school and share their ideas about what made a good learning environment.

DOI: 10.4324/9781003229988-7

They produced the following list:

A place to be me

- Somewhere you can be yourself.
- A place where you can be in your own little world.
- Somewhere you do not have to impress everybody.
- Somewhere where there are no limits to what you can do.
- Somewhere you can be proud of who you are.
- Somewhere you can learn in your own way.

It is important to note that they did not talk about the fabric of the building, the type or quantity of resources and facilities. They were much more concerned about how the learning environment made them feel. There is an old saying that children may forget what you said, but they will never forget how you made them feel. It is a good starting point when considering how to set up a space in which to share the books and it might be a useful exercise to carry out a similar survey with each cohort as they reflect on their own learning environments. The responses may vary depending on the child's experience of learning and ability to articulate their thoughts.

Some examples of personalised nurturing spaces are shown in the photographs shown in Figures 6.1–6.8.

Figure 6.1 A sensory stimulus.

Figure 6.2 A world of light.

Figure 6.3 An outdoor pathway.

Figure 6.4 A den in the forest.

Figure 6.5 A network of friends.

Figure 6.6 A construction stimulus.

Figure 6.7 A space story builder.

Figure 6.8 A forest hideaway.

A Place to be Me!
Enabling Environments

A physical or a mental space where the child feels safe and secure.

The space can be created inside or outside, a place to be alone or to hide away with friends. It might be a temporary den or a permanent structure.

Involve the child in making the space comfortable, find out what they need and what makes them feel relaxed and happy.

- **Observe the child**
  What kind of spaces does the child enjoy?

- **Create a space**
  Make an enclosed, covered space to talk and play.

- **Role play game**
  Put on a pair of golden wellies and imagine where you might go.

- **Design a place of your own:**
  Make an enclosed, covered space to talk and play.

Figure 6.9 Creating space. A place to be me.

7. Nurturing relationships

A key person who is effective in communication understands how to listen to a child and is responsive, flexible and positive. The key person does not have to be a trained specialist and could be a parent, carer, grandparent or older sibling. Introducing a new person at a time when a child is feeling vulnerable is not helpful; the child will respond best to someone they already know and trust, someone who they are willing and able to participate in 'serve and return' interactions (Figure 7.1).

Educators of non-verbal children emphasised the importance of an effective 'serve and return' communication system in helping to develop a nurturing relationship with each child. If communication systems such as signing, Makaton and Picture Exchange Communication Systems (PECS) are not used by the children it becomes much more difficult to find ways to develop this nurturing relationship. There is a need for the designated person, the educator, parent or carer to set up a communication system that can be used effectively by the child and the whole cohort to enable the child to make friends and build relationships.

Gaining an understanding of the importance of communication from an early age will only be achieved when a child's early attempts at communicating are valued and acted upon. A child who has experienced adverse early childhood trauma may have missed opportunities to connect with another person through the smallest of gestures, vocalisations or body language. It is these early experiences of connection that help a young child to see that they have a 'voice' and that their 'voice' (whether it is a sign, gesture, word or an action) can influence events and have impact. A familiar adult or key person who takes on the role of 'reflector' and 'facilitator' during interactions can be of real benefit to the child.

Early educators are often viewed by the child as trusted adults, so the child will share personal information and may sometimes disclose something important during a conversation. There can be a 'shared nervousness' within this nurturing relationship that sometimes gets in the way of open dialogue. The adult may feel anxiety about how to respond, what terms to use and what actions to take. In a similar way, the child may feel nervous about how the adult will respond, who they might tell or how they will react to what is said. Acknowledging this 'shared nervousness' in a relationship can be an important step in breaking down barriers that get in the way of open, honest conversation. A regular or daily check-in with the child may be all that is needed to overcome this anxiety – 'How are you doing?' 'Is everything OK?' or 'I'm here if you feel like talking to someone'.

Education in an emergency, when schools are closed or there is a shift to online learning, must consider the importance of face-to-face interaction and communication. The loss of non-verbal communication which can arise when learning takes place remotely will impact negatively on young children and especially those with sensory difficulties. Provision must always be made to address the need for nurturing and responsive relationships which run alongside an online digital solution.

DOI: 10.4324/9781003229988-8

The book *Someone to Listen* provides an opportunity to talk about how relationships are formed and how friendships can grow, working together on a shared vision, or in this case a shared garden, creating space to build relationships and find new friends. The child can explore in a safe space what it feels like to feel 'alone' in a crowded place and what the characters in the book might be feeling at different points in the story. The book could encourage children to participate in physical, outdoor activities such as planting seeds, digging a flower bed or planting an allotment: activities that promote engagement and participation in a group and a shared space in which to build relationships and encourage conversation.

Someone to Listen!
Enabling Environments

An audience for the child. A key person who will listen without judgement.

Someone who notices when a child wants to interact and communicate and who can facilitate a conversation alongside play.

Someone who gets down to the child's level, interacting, responding and extending the child's vocal sounds, mirroring actions and words.

- **Observe the child**
What kind of play does the child enjoy?

- **Total Communication**
Use signs, gestures and pictures to encourage conversation.

- **Joint attention**
Create a garden, go for a walk, play a game and let the child lead the interaction.

- **Make time to listen**
Rhythms and routines need to be flexible to give time to listen.

Get down to my level and make eye contact

Notice what I'm looking at and what I'm interested in

Give physical contact and reassurance

Give me time to play and talk alongside you

Smile and let me know it's good to talk!

Figure 7.1 Finding friends. Someone to listen.

8. Nurturing conversations

The dialogue between adults and children is a key element of effective learning – the classrooms of effective learners 'buzz' with conversation as children experiment with language and expression (Figure 8.1).

The use of Professor Laura Lundy's space, voice, audience and influence model at a key point of vulnerability such as transition into a school, or even an unexpected move to remote/home learning provides a framework for early intervention which is developmentally appropriate for a young child.

Adults actively open up new possibilities when they support the child through a period of change, reframing the memories for a child at risk of emotional imbalance due to past, negative experiences. Playful learning experiences can help a child to develop and practise a change or shift in stress response, which could be applied to new situations, helping to develop new coping mechanisms which can be repeated in times of high stress in future.

The model of participation appears to be naturally embedded within the teaching and learning styles of early years educators where children thrive. Given the scale of current political, media and public interest and the investment in mental health, there are new reasons to recommend a participatory approach to early education. An early education curriculum framework with four key elements – space, voice, audience and influence when children start school.

Nurturing, participatory conversations can be started by open-ended questioning and commentary relating to a shared experience – such as reading a book together. Young children are familiar with this approach and will not feel threatened especially when the adult reader is familiar to them and has their trust. Educators encourage conversation with a young child using open-ended, non-threatening questioning phrases which can be used across different situations:

> I wonder if …
> Tell me about …
> What do you think …?
> I wonder why …
> I am curious to know …

Conversation, dialogue and commentary can be used effectively to encourage a growth mindset, building on the power of 'not yet'. Children see the characters in a picture book or role-play story as failing, feeling

DOI: 10.4324/9781003229988-9

scared, changing their minds and learning from their experiences. The child learns that it is 'normal' to make mistakes, they gain an understanding that change can be good and that changes occur as they get more information or listen to others. Children are encouraged to look at the illustrations, and through a nurturing conversation add their own thoughts and ideas.

The key features of a nurturing conversation whilst sharing a story are that there is an open, trusting relationship that develops between participants; there are opportunities to both talk and to listen, taking turns to react and respond to each other. Nurturing conversations are reflective, so there needs to be' thinking time and children must have the freedom to change their minds in response to what they have heard or as their thinking develops.

Children need to know their 'voice' has been heard, what they have expressed is valued and will be acted upon. Listening to the child reduces levels of stress and anxiety, the child is no longer 'fighting' to be heard. The educator and the child move towards a much more constructive, participatory conversation and positive relationship.

The picture book which focuses on 'speaking out – a voice of my own' demonstrates to both children and adults how easy it can be to interpret a non-verbal communication system using gestures, pictures and signs. Children are encouraged to notice and talk about non-verbal cues, an opportunity to actively listen and respond to the many different voices of the characters in the picture books. Having a 'voice' can mean different things to different people, it might look and sound different wherever you are in the world and whoever you are with. The signs, pictures and words become a 'voice' when someone else listens and acts on what has been said. We give people a 'voice' by listening to what they have to say – this takes time and effort on behalf of the listener but is in line with Article 12 of the United Nations Convention on the Rights of the Child (UNCRC); we have a responsibility to give children their 'voice' in all matters affecting them.

SUPPORT MATERIAL

A Voice of My Own!
Enabling Environments

A system for communication which is well understood by everyone.

Play and participation is made possible when a child is able to communicate. A child needs someone to communicate with and something to communicate about.

Notice if the child is able to express their ideas, thoughts and feelings. Are they able to make choices, make mistakes and change their minds!

- **Observe the child**
How does the child choose to communicate?

- **Non- verbal Communication**
Be aware of what you are communicating through your hands, face and posture.

- **Role play games**
Use mime, drama, music and art to practice different forms of expression without words.

- **Choice Boards/Now & Next**
Use visual support to give structured choices and explain routines.

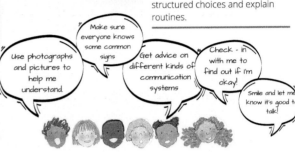

Use photographs and pictures to help me understand

Make sure everyone knows some common signs

Get advice on different kinds of communication systems

Check - in with me to find out if I'm okay!

Smile and let me know it's good to talk!

Figure 8.1 Speaking out. A voice of my own.

9. A change in the balance of power

When young children are given space, encouraged to use their voice with people who are ready to listen and act on what they say, they learn that it is good to communicate, it is good to talk. One child described it as 'a place to be me' and this provided the catalyst to find out more about what children think and what they need (Figure 9.1).

When children are given a sense of agency at a key point of potential vulnerability such as transition into school, or moving from one place to another, it provides a framework for mental health early intervention which is developmentally appropriate. Adults use playful learning experiences and storytelling to develop and practise a change or shift in stress response, which the child can then apply to new situations. Children could test out different responses in a safe and familiar space, in school or at home with adults whom they trust.

By reframing the memories and experiences for a child at risk of mental health difficulties, the adults actively open new possibilities which children are happy to embrace. The use of picture books, child-friendly words and images to show coping mechanisms and describe practical strategies, enables a young child in the future to recall and make use of similar actions in times of high stress. The familiarity of the picture book characters and contexts allows young children to identify with the characters, sharing their own ideas about what might happen next and why. The act of 'stepping into another person's shoes' to think about what the character might be feeling is an important skill for young children to practise.

This shift in the balance of power is an important experience for a child who may never have had an opportunity to have an influence on the world around them. The child who felt powerless to act, learns that they do have a say in what happens next, and that what they think, feel and 'voice' matters.

Continuous provision in a classroom provides the young child with autonomy over their own learning environment – the child chooses where to go, what to do and has the freedom to move between continuous provision areas and activities. The layout and organisation of resources in an early years classroom or learning 'space' should promote autonomy and independence. The child is encouraged and sometimes challenged to make choices – learning that they can decide, change their mind, get it wrong or get it right! They can rehearse the decision-making process in a safe environment with familiar, trusted adults. A classroom layout where all the decisions are made by the adults does not develop a growth mindset, it does not build mental health competencies and is not developmentally appropriate for younger children.

DOI: 10.4324/9781003229988-10

During school closures there has been a misconception that remote learning involves sitting at a table or desk whilst the adult, parent, carer or even the computer directs the child to learn. Unfortunately, images on social media and in the press have reinforced this view of education and this is particularly detrimental to early years practice where playful learning across an entire range of situations is important. This is further complicated by the recent, rapid increase in online learning platforms – one solution to enable children to access teaching and learn remotely but which must be seen as just one of many tools used for remote learning. Opportunities for 'live' interaction and communication are limited within an online educational programme and there is a risk that the child becomes passive in their approach to learning: 'Tell me what you want me to do, and I'll do it'. Many opportunities to extend a child's thinking, talking, and questioning during the learning process will be missed and there is a real risk that learning becomes more about completing a finished product rather than an interactive process.

When children are given open-ended materials – a set of wooden blocks or recycled building materials (tin cans, boxes, stones and sticks) there will be much greater scope for autonomy and independence. The child decides what to use, how to use it and how to make changes to improve the construction. The child invests time and energy, often building a narrative alongside their play. Radio programmes, role-play and storytelling may be the most effective way of developing this kind of approach when a parent or carer is supporting education remotely or at home. It is important to recognise that when schools are closed, the digital learning tools used in early childhood education become far more effective when a key person is on hand to interact and play – an older sibling or grandparent can act as a 'learning partner' for a young child and then the digital tool becomes a much more effective solution for remote early learning.

Early educators who are concerned about children's mental health and wellbeing need to continue to be strong advocates for active play-based learning at home and in school. Mental health competencies are nurtured by learning through play (LtP) approaches. A shift towards more formal approaches in early education is detrimental to a young child's freedom to think, to play and to talk. If children are exposed to formal learning at an early age, when the plasticity of the brain is most malleable then there will be missed opportunities to notice and change how a child responds to challenges. The child may struggle to learn how to restore the balance and regulate their own behaviours when overwhelmed with emotions, unless a trusted adult is available to notice, model and offer help. When children learn through play, they are learning important mental health competencies that will form the foundations for the future – the child is learning to confidently ask for help when they need it, they will recognise adults they can trust, form friendships, build relationships, make mistakes, make decisions, change their mind, work alongside others, and articulate their thoughts and feelings.

We can't prevent children from reaching a crisis point later in life, but we can equip them with the vocabulary and capability to seek help when it is needed. Asking for help is a key skill that should be encouraged from an early age, creating an environment where help-seeking is a natural part of the daily routine, whether it is help from adults or from peers. In effect we are building a community around young children that understands the value of 'help-seeking'. It is an intervention strategy that involves shifting the balance of power, allowing a young child to lead the play and conversation, choosing when they need help and when they don't.

Memories of Change!
Nurturing Environments

Creating positive memories of 'being heard' and 'knowing you matter' will help a child to feel empowered to seek help and engage with others.

The child learns that change can be good, that an unexpected event or experience can turn into something positive.

The child is encouraged to recognise and name their feelings, noticing how others are impacted and how these feelings can change over time and when we work together.

- **Observe the child**
How does the child react to change?

- **Now & Next / Whoops Card**
Support changes in the daily routine with pictures and words.

- **Multi sensory play**
Use clay, play dough, paint and cooking activities to talk about change.

- **Changes in nature**
Focus on change and transitions in nature - lifecycles, the seasons and growth.

Figure 9.1 Thinking differently. Memories of change.

10. Practical actions

The collection of data which describes the mental health of a generation of children starting school can be collated at low cost, building on existing practice in UK schools and managed in a way that is least intrusive for the child. The key person becomes an action researcher collecting information from their observations that inform and shape their own practice with each child.

There are four key points for practical action that can be easily implemented when setting up an enabling and nurturing environment. These four areas can provide core themes when planning sensitive interactions that will protect a child's mental health and wellbeing. These have been translated into child-friendly picture books which can be used to elicit nurturing conversations with a young child. The child is encouraged to look, think aloud, talk and connect with others following up the ideas in their play.

Create space – a place of my own

Young children learn how to describe a physical or mental space that makes them feel happy, secure, excited or curious. Thinking, imagining and talking about a place where a child feels happy and secure can be helpful when responding to stress or anxiety in the future. The child can choose to return to that place of safety in their imagination or they can recreate it in their play. Describing a visual image through playful interaction, drawing or painting a picture which is unique and feels special to the child can become a useful tool for the future. This picture book is used to stimulate conversation in which a child can begin to describe a real or imaginary space; a child might describe it as 'a place of my own' and could be encouraged to reflect on why that place has special meaning for them (Figure 10.1).

Describing a physical 'space' that meets the needs of each child can be supported by a key person who knows the child well, someone who observes and 'notices' the child's levels of wellbeing, involvement and interests daily. The educators in this study often created a 'space' in their learning environments using familiar objects (fabric, cushions, favourite books) – a place where the child could feel safe. Sometimes, children chose their own spaces and were supported to help create and embellish the space. For example, a child who frequently hides under a table or hides in a corner needs an enclosed space in that location to feel 'at home', whilst a child who likes to lose themselves in small world play needs a quiet play space with access to open-ended small world resources to build their own narratives as they play. The role of the adult is to notice where the child chooses to go to relax or reduce stress and to be flexible enough to allocate that space as an area to encourage self-regulation.

The picture book was adapted from a project carried out with a reception class which had recently started school. The story of the 'golden wellies' encourages children to describe their own space – an imaginary

DOI: 10.4324/9781003229988-11

Figure 10.1 Create space – *A Place of My Own*.

place or a memory. Children (and adults) are given the freedom to play with their imagination, using language to describe, enhance and question as they build a visual picture for themselves and each other. Characters in the story model different possibilities; a child who is experiencing a sense of loss may describe a place from the past recalling familiar events, people and experiences. A child who is feeling nervous about a move to a new place can begin to envisage what the change might be like. It is important to remember there are no right or wrong answers; the child takes control of the conversation and steers the interaction. The adult's role is to listen, model the thinking process, sensitively asking questions and reflecting back to help build the picture.

Finding out about each child's special place can also help when setting up a learning environment or when setting the scene for a nurturing conversation. As children listen to each other they are learning more about themselves and each other, rehearsing a visualisation process that can be repeated in times of stress. Children learn that having a special place is important for everyone, and each person needs something that's different.

In this picture book, a pair of golden wellies provide the mode of transport to get to that special place – a potential gateway to a whole series of adventures and expeditions that might follow on from reading the book. In the original school project that was the inspiration for the book, further role-play was stimulated when a pair of 'golden wellington boots' was placed in the classroom prompting children's curiosity, exchanging ideas and engaging in imaginative play. The characters in the story are encouraged to take a 'risk', one by one each child in the reception class participated, putting on the golden wellies and telling their own 'story' about where they found themselves. The children involved in the original project embarked on a line of inquiry that sparked their interest, one which lasted the whole term.

Speak out – a voice of my own

Young children learn to listen, not only with their ears but making use of all their senses. All the characters in this picture book are communicating something important and they rely on others to interpret meaning from their gestures, actions, interactions and their voices. The illustrations require the readers to look carefully and try to work out what the characters are saying to them. Children are encouraged to consider why giving everyone a 'voice' and listening to each other is important and they are given an opportunity to actively listen to different kinds of 'voices'. The pictures and text prompt discussion about how it feels when no-one is listening, or when you are misunderstood. Identifying what the book characters are trying to communicate will lead to a shared understanding of the importance of finding your own 'voice' and how you use it to communicate effectively with others taking time to listen to each other (Figure 10.2).

Figure 10.2 Speaking out – *A Voice of My Own*.

Participation at home and in an educational setting becomes much more possible when a child has an effective communication system – someone to communicate *with* and something to communicate *about*. A child who is taught to sign needs others who can interpret those signs for it to be effective as a communicative exchange. When vulnerable children start school, it is vital to look for the different forms of expression that could be used by that child to communicate and provide lots of opportunities for the child to try out different forms of expression across every area of the learning environment. Any communication system that allows children to express their ideas and thoughts, likes and dislikes, to make choices and decisions gives a child a feeling of empowerment.

The picture book is designed to show various kinds of communication, helping children to consider how to listen, interpret and respond appropriately. The book encourages audience participation, guessing the intentions of each character, wondering about the consequences if the communication is misunderstood, linking it to first-hand experiences. Children learn that communication is important and that everyone has the right to express themselves and be understood.

When children reflect on their own use of communication, including reliance on the use of non-verbal cues, sign language and pictures they can begin to consider what gets in the way of effective communication between people. They begin to understand what can happen when communication breaks down. Having a 'voice' is a human right which requires someone to 'listen' (an audience) to make it effective. Young children, particularly those who have been subject to early trauma may feel 'voiceless', they may find they are unable to communicate effectively, and their behaviours and actions are frequently misunderstood. Having an opportunity to discuss how you can use a communication system (a voice, a picture or signs) will be especially important for a child who may need to ask for help but also for those who may want to offer help. Having the ability to articulate feelings at an early age is an important skill that will benefit a young person who may need to describe their feelings at a later stage in life.

Find friends – someone to listen

The importance of a key person willing and open to listen without judgement should not be underestimated. There are many reasons why a community around a young child may not respond in this way. In a global pandemic the focus has been on social rather than physical distancing, the immense social and economic pressures on adults and school closures meant that a child's circle of friends and relatives has significantly reduced. Finding someone who has the time and inclination to listen became more difficult for some children and this had a direct effect on their mental health.

This picture book highlights the importance of having an audience, someone to listen to you. The child considers how characters might be feeling at different points in the book. Children are encouraged to notice the shift in the feelings of the characters as the reader moves through the book – children begin to

articulate what it is that makes the characters feel more valued, what makes the characters slow down and take time to talk. Relating the different experiences of the characters to their own lives, children consider what they need to flourish and thrive within their own community (Figure 10.3).

Someone who 'notices' what you are feeling and has power to act on your behalf is an important way in which educators of young children model empathy. It requires a key person, someone who is tuned into the child, such as a parent, grandparent or sibling. An educator who knows the child well and who is trained to actively listen is someone who is willing to get down to the child's level, interacting, responding and reacting to what the child says, thinks and does. Where you see adults who can mirror, comment, reflect and respond to the child's actions, vocal sounds and words alongside their play they are building a child's resilience through sensitive interaction.

While curiosity is the driving force that underpins the actions of characters in the picture book, the 'other side' of curiosity is anxiety, which provides a natural caution that is a safety net when trying something new. When curiosity propels us towards new discoveries, so anxiety hold us back. When the two are in healthy balance then action is 'bold, sensible and pleasurable'. This push/pull emotional seesaw is natural and will continue to influence our actions and responses throughout life.

Figure 10.3 Finding friends – *Someone to Listen.*

It is only when adults 'stand back, watch and wonder' that they really see the possibilities for each child. The idea that a child is already a 'confident, competent learner' from birth and that even the youngest of children can exercise their human rights.

The UN Sustainability Goals and UNESCO Education for Sustainable Development provides a stark reminder for all educators working with children and young people about our responsibilities:

- **Working in non-discriminatory ways (Article 2):**
  a child has rights whatever their race or skin colour, whether boy, girl or other, whatever language is spoken, whatever religion, political beliefs, nationality or ethnic group, whether rich or poor, and whether the child is disabled.
- **Working in the best interest of the child (Article 3):**
  whenever adults make decisions or do anything that affects the child, they should always think about what is best for him/her.
- **Providing the right to life, survival and healthy development (Article 6):**
  the child has the right to live, learn and develop holistically. The government should make sure a child has the chance to survive and develop healthily.
- **Providing for the right to be heard (Article 12):**
  when important decisions are being made that affect the child, he/she has the right to give an opinion and to be taken seriously.
- **Providing for the right to play (Article 31):**
  all children have the right to rest, play and take part in cultural and artistic activities.

Reflecting on the ways in which a child's human rights are implemented within local communities, educational settings and families is a useful topic for discussion. The picture book encourages a discussion to take place amongst children using developmentally appropriate language and illustrations.

Think differently – memories of change

A young child may not feel able to make decisions and may not recognise their 'ability' to change the world around them. This book was created working together with children and an artist-in-residence and tracks the 'journey' in thinking as children engage in a role-play narrative. The story and actions of children in the book are typical of any group of children but it is the process and changes in thinking that are important as they engage in the game. The children conclude that their imaginary 'apple crumble machine' cannot work, but they do not give up. They start again, they change their ideas, they collaborate and experiment and when they do, the outcomes change for them. There is a shift in the way they are thinking that opens new possibilities and new ways of working, allowing them to see the world differently (Figure 10.4).

Figure 10.4 Think differently – *Memories of Change*.

Transition is about 'change' and any change will provide a crucial opportunity for learning as children develop and establish their memories of change. The transition experience can create a positive memory or a negative memory for a child depending on what has happened in the past. Vulnerable children are likely to have experienced more changes in their lives than their peers so turning these difficult memories into positive memories of change is even more important for these children. When vulnerable children start school, they may have already started to embed negative memories of transition and change: between home and hospital, moving to a new house, moving between one culture to another. The educator needs to consider the memories of transition already embedded in a child's brain and look for ways to address negative memories. Now, more than ever it will be important to reframe a child's memories of events during the pandemic. Helping a child to talk through the 'process' of thinking and recognising that thinking patterns can change over time will help to build resilience for the future. The aim is to shift the memory to focus on the positive, something that empowers the child and gives a feeling of autonomy. The practical application of participatory pedagogy across education will help to shift the balance of power, empowering children to manage feelings and self-regulate from an early age.

The story of the apple crumble machine was written by a group of children in a primary school. As they built the narrative alongside their role-play, they began to realise they all had a need to make changes to the way they were working together. The book tells the story of their special machine but also demonstrates the importance of stopping to reflect, recognising when something is not working and if necessary, starting again. The apple crumble machine only works when the group of children listen to each other, and changes are made – in this scenario the children are in charge and the changes they decide to make are all that is needed to get the machine working.

Helping young children to see the value of stopping, waiting, reflecting and reviewing, are all valuable skills that can be applied to many situations throughout life. It may come naturally to some children but for those that frequently fall into a fight, freeze or flight mode it may need to be rehearsed through playful conversation and role-play.

Appendix 1
Glossary

Mental health: Mental health is defined as a state of wellbeing in which every individual realises his or her own potential, can cope with the normal stresses of life, can work productively and fruitfully and is able to make a contribution to her or his community (World Health Organization, 2004).

Mental health difficulty: Mental health problems range from worries to serious long-term conditions. When a child experiences a mental health difficulty this is often visible in their behaviours and in their interactions with others.

Mental health competence: Positive mental health, thriving, flourishing or wellbeing, healthy psychosocial functioning. Competences in this study included a sense of wellbeing, involvement, curiosity, symbolic play, focus, concentration, a sense of achievement, ability to make links, build relationships, interact and communicate.

Vulnerable: A child in this study was identified as vulnerable if they had met the criteria in their school to be formally registered as SEND, EAL or Pupil Premium. This represents a much narrower understanding of vulnerability than is generally used which was appropriate for the purposes of this research only.

Disadvantage: Any child who may experience an unfavourable circumstance or condition that reduces or limits their chance of success or effectiveness. The absence of equality which may set limits or barriers to learning.

Participative pedagogy: A pedagogical approach in which the child is encouraged to find their own voice to express their thoughts and emotions, an opportunity for the child to examine the relationships and environments that support learning from different perspectives.

Listening pedagogy: The openness and sensitivity to listen and be listened to – listening not just with our ears, but with all of our senses (sight, touch, smell, taste, orientation). Listening needs time – time to be silent, to pause and to listen to ourselves.

Special educational rights: Specialist provision that enables a child to participate, learn and make progress. An acceptance and celebration of different ways of learning and of different ways of being.

Special educational needs and disability (SEND): A child or young person has SEND if they have a learning difficulty or disability which calls for special educational provision to be made for him or her.

Pupil Premium (PP): The Pupil Premium is additional funding which is allocated to schools on the basis of the number of pupils who have been eligible for free school meals (FSM) at any point over the last six years (known as 'Ever 6 FSM') and service children, including those who were eligible for the Service Child Premium at any point in the last three years. Students in care, who have been looked after by local authorities for more than six months, also continue to qualify for the Pupil Premium. The Pupil Premium is aimed at addressing the current underlying inequalities which exist between children from disadvantaged backgrounds and their more affluent peers.

English as an additional language (EAL): A learner of English as an additional language (EAL) is a pupil whose first language is other than English. A first language is the language to which the child was initially exposed during early development and continues to use this language in the home and community. If a child acquires English subsequent to early development, then English is not their first language no matter how proficient in it they become.

Bibliography

Allen, G. (2011) *Early intervention: The next steps. An independent report to Her Majesty's Government*. http://www.grahamallenmp.co.uk/static/pdf/early-intervention-7th.pdf

Australian Early Development Census (2018) https://www.aedc.gov.au/. First Accessed January 2018.

Bayrampour, H., Fraser-Lee, N., Kehler, H. L., McDonald, S. W. and Tough, S. (2016) Risk and protective factors for early child development: Results from the all our babies (AOB) pregnancy cohort. *British Medical Journal Open* 6: e012096. doi:10.1136/bmjopen-2016-012096

Bertram, T. and Pascal, C. (2013) *The impact of early education as a strategy in countering socio-economic disadvantage*. Centre for Research into Early Childhood (CREC), Office for Standards in Education (Ofsted). http://www.crec.co.uk/docs/Access.pdf

Brinkman, S. A., Carr, V., Gialamas, A., Goldfeld, S., Gregory, T., Hertzman, C., Janus, M., Lynch, J., Mittinty, M. N., Rahman, A., Silburn, S. and Zubrick, S. (2012) Jurisdictional, socioeconomic and gender inequalities in child health and development: Analysis of a national census of 5-year-olds in Australia. *BMJ Open* 2: e001075. doi:10.1136/bmjopen-2012-001075

Brownlie, E. B., Bao, L. and Beitchman, J. (2016) Childhood language disorder and social anxiety in early adulthood. *Journal of Abnormal Child Psychology* 44: 1061. doi:10.1007/s10802-015-0097-5

Carpenter, H., Papps, I., Bragg, J., Dyson, A., Harris, D., Kerr, K., Todd, L. and Laing, K. (2013) *Evaluation of pupil premium research report*. Research Report DFE-RR282 TNS BMRB, TECIS, Centre for Equity in Education, University of Manchester and Newcastle University. http://dera.ioe.ac.uk/18010/1/DFE-RR282.pdf

Carter, A. S., Briggs-Gowan, M. J. and Davis, N. O. (2004) Assessment of young children's social-emotional development and psychopathology: Recent advances and recommendations for practice. *Journal of Child Psychology and Psychiatry* 45: 109–134. doi:10.1046/j.0021-9630.2003.00316.x

Center on the Developing Child. (2013) *Early childhood mental health* (InBrief). https://developingchild.harvard.edu/resources/inbrief-early-childhood-mental-health/

Chen, F. (2015) Parents' and children's emotion regulation strategies in emotionally situated zones: A cultural historical perspective. *Australasian Journal of Early Childhood* 40(2): 107–116. https://www.researchgate.net/publication/280318871_Parents%27_and_children%27s_emotion_regulation_strategies_in_emotionally_situated_zones_A_cultural-historical_perspective

Children's Commission (2017) *On measuring the number of vulnerable children in England*. Children's Commissioner for England. http://www.childrenscommissioner.gov.uk/wp-content/uploads/2017/07/CCO-On-vulnerability-Overveiw-2.pdf

Christensen, D., Fahey, M. T., Giallo, R. and Hancock, K. J. (2017) Longitudinal trajectories of mental health in Australian children aged 4–5 to 14–15 years. *PLoS ONE* 12(11): e0187974. doi:10.1371/journal.pone.0187974

Clark, M. (2005) *Understanding Research in Early Education: The Relevance for the Future of Lessons from the Past.* Third edition. Oxon: Routledge.

Cooperrider, D. and Whitney, D. (2018) *Appreciative inquiry global community of practice.* https://appreci ativeinquiry.champlain.edu/learn/appreciative-inquiry-introduction/

Coram Voice (2015) *Measuring well-being: A literature review.* Hadley Centre for Adoption and Foster Studies. http://www.coramvoice.org.uk/sites/default/files/Measuring%20Wellbeing%20FINAL.pdf

Cremeens, J., Eiser, C. and Blades, M. (2006) Characteristics of health-related self-report measures for children aged three to eight years: A review of the literature. *Quality of Life Research* 15(4): 739–54. doi:10.1007/s11136-005-4184-x

Cremeens, J., Eiser, C. and Blades, M. (2007) Brief report: Assessing the impact of rating scale type, types of items, and age on the measurement of school-age children's self-reported quality of life. *Journal of Paediatric Psychology* 32(2): 132–138. doi:10.1093/jpepsy/jsj119. https://www.researchgate.net/public ation/7155507_Brief_Report_Assessing_the_Impact_of_Rating_Scale_Type_Types_of_Items_and_Ag e_on_the_Measurement_of_School-Age_Children%27s_Self-Reported_Quality_of_Life

Dan, A. (2016) Supporting and developing self-regulatory behaviours in early childhood in young children with high levels of impulsive behaviour. *Contemporary Issues in Education Research (Online)* 9(4): 189–200. https://eric.ed.gov/?id=EJ1116432

Early Intervention Foundation (2013) http://www.eif.org.uk/. First Accessed December 2017.

Egger, H. L. and Angold, A. (2006) Common emotional and behavioral disorders in preschool children: Presentation, nosology, and epidemiology. *Journal of Child Psychology and Psychiatry* 47(3–4): 313–337. https://www.ncbi.nlm.nih.gov/pubmed/16492262

Erwin, E. J., Brotherson, M. and Summers, J. A. (2011) Understanding qualitative metasynthesis, issues and opportunities in early childhood intervention and research. *Journal of Early Intervention* 33(3): 186–200. doi:10.1177/1053815111425493

Field, F. (2010) *The Foundation Years: Preventing Poor Children Becoming Poor Adults. The Report of the Independent Review on Poverty and Life Chances.* London: Cabinet Office.

Formosinho, J. and Oliveira-Formosinho, J. (2012) Towards a social science of the social: The contribution of praxeological research. *European Early Childhood Education Research Journal* 20(4). https://www.res earchgate.net/publication/263247850_Towards_a_social_science_of_the_social_The_contribution_ of_praxeological_research

Gapminder Foundation. (2005) https://www.gapminder.org/. First Accessed December 2018.

Goodman, A. and Goodman, R. (2009) Strengths and difficulties questionnaire as a dimensional measure of child mental health. *Journal of the American Academy of Child and Adolescent Psychiatry* 48(4): 400–3. doi:10.1097/CHI.0b013e3181985068

Green, H., McGinnity, A., Meltzer, H., Ford, T. and Goodman, R. (2011) *No Health Without Mental Health. A Cross Government Mental Health Outcomes Strategy for People of all Ages. Analysis of the Impact of Quality. A Survey Carried Out by the Department of Health.* Basingstoke: Palgrave Macmillan.

H.M Government (2017) *Transforming children and young people's mental health provision: A green paper.* https://www.gov.uk/government/consultations/transforming-children-and-young-peoples-mental-health -provision-a-green-paper

Layard, R. and Hagall, A. (2015) *Healthy young minds: Transforming the mental health of children.* Report of the WISH Mental Health and Wellbeing in Children Forum. Qatar: World Innovation Summit in Health.

Layous, K., Chancellor, J. and Lyubomirsky, S. (2014) Positive activities as protective factors against mental health conditions. *Journal of Abnormal Psychology* 123(1): 3–12.

Lloyd, K. and Emerson, L. (2016) (Re)examining the relationship between children's subjective wellbeing and their perceptions of participation rights. *Child Indicators Research* 10: 591–608. doi:10.1007/s12187-016-9396-9

Longfield, A. (2021) While calls for help about child abuse increase, 600,000 vulnerable children remain invisible to the state. *TheHouse.* https://www.politicshome.com/thehouse/article/child-abuse-increase-invisble-covid-19

Love, P. and Ellis, J. (2018) *Knowledge sharing, learning and situated practice: Communities of practice for projects.* https://www.researchgate.net/publication/242103252_KNOWLEDGE_SHARING_LEARNING _AND_SITUATED_PRACTICE_COMMUNITIES_OF_PRACTICE_FOR_PROJECTS

Lundy, L. (2007) 'Voice' is not enough: Conceptualising article 12 of the United Nations convention on the rights of the child. *British Educational Research Journal* 33(6): 927–942. https://www.researchgate.net /publication/248994859_%27Voice%27_is_not_enough_Conceptualising_Article_12_of_the_United _Nations_Convention_on_the_Rights_of_the_Child

Male, T. and Palaiologou, I. (2013) Pedagogical leadership in the 21st century: Evidence from the field. *Educational Management Administration and Leadership.* Sage Publications. http://journals.sagepub.com /doi/abs/10.1177/1741143213494889

Mannay, D. (2016) *Visual, Narrative and Creative Research Methods: Application, Reflection and Ethics.* First edition. Oxon: Routledge.

Marryat, L., Thompson, L., Minnis, H. and Wilson, P. (2018) Primary schools and the amplification of social differences in child mental health: A population-based cohort study. *Journal of Epidemiology and Community Health* 72(1): 27–33. doi: 10.1136/jech-2017-208995

McCormack, J. M. and Verdon, S. E. (2015) Mapping speech pathology services to developmentally vulnerable and at-risk communities using the Australian early development census. *International Journal of Speech-Language Pathology* 17(3): 273–286.

Meltzer, H., Gatward, R., Goodman, R. and Ford, T. (2003) Mental health of children and adolescents in Great Britain. *International Review of Psychiatry* 15(1–2): 185–187. https://www.ncbi.nlm.nih.gov/p ubmed/12745331

Mental Health Foundation (2018) https://www.mentalhealth.org.uk/a-to-z/c/children-and-young-people. First Accessed June 2018.

Messenger, C. and Molloy, D. (2014) *Getting it right for families. Review of integrated systems and promising practice in the early years.* Early Intervention Foundation. http://www.eif.org.uk/wp-content/ uploads/2014/11/GETTING-IT-RIGHT-FULL-REPORT.pdf

NICE (National Institute for Health and Care Excellence) (2018) https://www.nice.org.uk/. First Accessed October 2017.

Ofsted (2016) *Unknown children – Destined for disadvantage?* Her Majesty's Chief Inspector of Schools, Ofsted. https://assets.publishing.service.gov.uk/government/uploads/system/uploads/attachment_data/file/541394/Unknown_children_destined_for_disadvantage.pdf

Ortlipp, M. (2008) *Keeping and using reflective journals in the qualitative research process.* https://www.researchgate.net/publication/228457846_Keeping_and_Using_Reflective_Journals_in_the_Qualitative_Research_Process

Parliamentary Select Committee Publications (2018) *The Government's green paper on mental health: Failing a generation.* https://publications.parliament.uk/pa/cm201719/cmselect/cmhealth/642/64210.htm#_idTextAnchor101

Pye, J., Lindley, L., Taylor, C., Evans, D. and Huxley, K. (2017) Evaluation of the pupil deprivation grant: Interim report (December 2015). *Social Research* 77/2017: 4–8.

Roberts, W. (2015) Enabling change through education for children and their families experiencing vulnerability and disadvantage: The understandings of early childhood professionals. *Australasian Journal of Early Childhood* 40: 49–56. https://www.researchgate.net/publication/282373897_Enabling_change_through_education_for_children_and_their_families_experiencing_vulnerability_and_disadvantage_The_understandings_of_early_childhood_professionals

Robson, C. and McCartan, K. (2017) *Real World Research.* Fourth edition. Chichester, UK: John Wiley & Sons Ltd.

Rouse, E. and O'Brien, D. (2017) Mutuality and reciprocity in parent-teacher relationships: Understanding the nature of partnerships in early childhood education and care provision. *Australian Journal of early Childhood* 42(2): 45–52. doi:10.23965/AJEC.42.2.06

Rowland, M. (2017) *Learning Without Labels Improving Outcomes for Vulnerable Pupils.* Melton, UK: John Catt Educational Ltd.

Sabates, R. and Dex, S. (2015) The impact of multiple risk factors on young children's cognitive and behavioural development. *Children & Society* 29: 95–108. doi:10.1111/chso.12024

Shonkoff, J. and Garner, A. (2011) The lifelong effects of early childhood adversity and toxic stress. *American Academy of Pediatrics* 129: e232–46. doi:10.1542/peds.2011-2663. http://pediatrics.aappublications.org/content/early/2011/12/21/peds.2011-2663

Sroufe, A. (1996) *Emotional Development: The Organization of Emotional Development in Early Years* (Cambridge Studies in Social and Emotional Development, pp. i–vi). Cambridge: Cambridge University Press. doi:10.1017/CBO9780511527661

Sylva, K., Melhuish, E., Sammons, P., Siraj, I. and Taggart, B. (1996–2016) *The Effective Pre-School, Primary and Secondary Education project (EPPSE).* http://www.education.ox.ac.uk/research/fell/research/effective-pre-school-primary-and-secondary-education/

Sylva, K., Melhuish, E., Sammons, P., Siraj-Blatchford, I. and Taggart, B. (eds). (2004) *The Effective Provision of Pre-School Education [EPPE] Project: Final Report.* London, UK: Institute of Education, University of London.

Szaniecki, E. and Barnes, J. (2016) Measurement issues: Measures of infant mental health. *Child Adolescent Mental Health* 21: 64–74. doi:10.1111/camh.12106

Taylor, C. (2017) The reliability of free school meal eligibility as a measure of socio-economic disadvantage: Evidence from the millennium cohort study in Wales. *British Journal of Educational Studies* 66(1): 29–51. doi:10.1080/00071005.2017.1330464

The Children's Society (n.d.) https://www.childrenssociety.org.uk/. First Accessed October 2017.

Tickell, C. (2011) *The early years: Foundations for life, health and learning.* An independent report on the early years foundation stage to Her Majesty's Government. https://assets.publishing.service.gov.uk/government/uploads/system/uploads/attachment_data/file/180919/DFE-00177-2011.pdf

Tol, W. A., Song, S. and Jordans, M. J. D. (2013) Annual research review: Resilience and mental health in children and adolescents living in areas of armed conflict – A systematic review of findings in low- and middle-income countries. *Journal Child Psychology and Psychiatry* 54: 445–460. doi:10.1111/jcpp.12053

Twenge, J. (2000) The age of anxiety? Birth cohort change in anxiety and neuroticism, 1952–1993. *Journal of Personality and Social Psychology* 79: 1007–1021. doi:10.1037//0022-3514.79.6.1007

Vaz, S., Cordier, R., Falkmer, M., Ciccarelli, M., Parsons, R., McAuliffe, T. and Falkmer, T. (2015) Should schools expect poor physical and mental health, social adjustment, and participation outcomes in students with disability? *PLoS ONE* 10(5): e0126630. doi:10.1371/journal.pone.0126630

Wichstrøm, L., Berg-Nielsen, T. S., Angold, A., Egger, H. L., Solheim, E. and Sveen, T. H. (2012) Prevalence of psychiatric disorders in preschoolers. *Journal of Child Psychology and Psychiatry* 53: 695–705. doi:10.1111/j.1469-7610.2011.02514.x

Wlodarczyk, O., Pawils, S. and Metzner, F. (2017) Risk and protective factors for mental health problems in preschool-aged children: Cross-sectional results of the BELLA preschool study. *Child and Adolescent Psychiatry and Mental Health* 11(1): 1.

Wlodarczyk, O., Schwarze, M., Rumpf, H.-J., Metzner, F. and Pawils, S. (2017) Protective mental health factors in children of parents with alcohol and drug use disorders: A systematic review. *PLoS ONE* 12(6): e0179140. doi:10.1371/journal.pone.0179140

Wood, N., Bann, D., Hardy, R., Gale, C., Goodman, A. and Crawford, C. (2017) Childhood socioeconomic position and adult mental wellbeing: Evidence from four British birth cohort studies. *PLoS ONE* 12(10): e0185798. doi:10.1371/journal.pone.0185798

World Health Organization. (2004) *Promoting mental health: Concepts, emerging evidence, practice (summary report).* Geneva: World Health Organization.

Youngminds (2018) https://youngminds.org.uk/. First Accessed October 2017.

Zentner, M., Smolkina, M. and Venables, P. (2014) Effects of measurement aggregation on predicting externalizing problems from preschool behaviour. *British Journal Developmental Psychology* 32: 468–479. doi:10.1111/bjdp.12059

Index

participation 13, 17–18, 27, 31–33, 44–46, 54

participatory pedagogy 8, 31–33, 57

pedagogy 33–36, 59

physical demeanour 18

plasticity of the brain 8, 49

play 1, 6–9, 14–19, 23–27, 29–36, 44–53, 55–58

primary School 9, 15, 37, 57

proximal development 17

realistic optimism 4

recovery 5

relationships 4–8, 13, 17–19, 31–34, 43–44, 49

remote learning 43, 45, 49

resilience 1, 4–5, 15, 20, 36, 55, 57

risk factors 12, 13, 15, 20,

role play 1, 6, 9, 15–19, 27, 30, 32–36, 45–46, 51–52, 56–58

safe space 1, 9, 27, 30, 32–35, 37, 44, 48–51

self-regulate 4, 7, 15, 57

self-regulation 4, 5, 15, 19

social stories 35, 36

space 14, 19, 23–35, 37–39, 44–45, 38, 51

special needs 7, 16, 32, 51–52, 54, 57; rights 6, 31–32, 59

storytelling 32, 36, 48–49

stress 1, 8, 14–15, 17, 23, 27, 30, 35–37, 45–48, 51–52; toxic 5–6

think differently 9, 38–39, 49, 56–57

transition 14–15, 45, 48–49, 57

trauma 5, 8, 12, 31, 43, 54

trust 13, 16, 43, 45, 48, 49

UNCRC 31, 46

visualisation 27, 30, 52

voice 9, 31–33, 43, 45–48, 53–54

vulnerability 7, 11–12, 45, 48, 59

wellbeing 1, 4–9, 13, 15–20, 23, 31–32, 35–37, 49–51

worry box 1

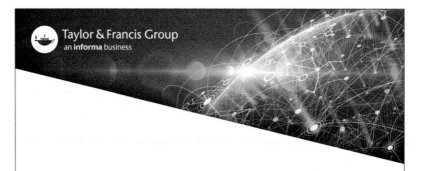